3510458251
UNIVERSITY OF LINCOLN
KT-418-507
Everything About Purchase, Care,
Nutrition, Behavior, and Housing
Filled with Full-color Photographs
Illustrations by Michele Earle-Bridges
BARRON'S

CONTENTS

INTRODUCTION TO THE DEGU

The soft, gentle animal with the large, bright eyes returns your gaze. It shares your curiosity and radiates intelligence. Unlike anything you've seen before, you lean closer to have a better look.

The Pocket Pet

Resembling a small squirrel with large ears and a tufted tail, the small creature sits up, sniffs the air, makes a low call in greeting, and awaits your next move. But you dare not stir for fear of losing the magic of the moment. Already you are mesmerized by this attractive little being, trapped by its charm, with a desire to learn more about it. This book will take you on an interesting journey into the secret life of one of the world's oldest, most fascinating, and most mysterious rodents—the degu. And once you discover what a wonderful companion a degu can be, and how it can enhance your life, you will no doubt be taking one home.

The degu is a "pocket pet," an affectionate term for companion animals tiny enough to fit into your pocket. A South American rodent, native to the western slopes of the Andes Mountains, degus can be found at elevations of 3,937 feet (1,200 m). It is the most common mammal in Chile, numbering more than 100 per acre. But such is not the case in North America and Europe, where the degu's increasing popularity has made it sometimes difficult to keep up the supply for the growing demand for this good-natured, affectionate pet.

Degus adapt easily to life in captivity if they have plenty of hiding spaces and proper care.

Degu Characteristics

Weighing only ½ ounce (14 g) at birth and gaining 6 to 10½ ounces (170–300 g) by the time it is fully grown, a degu will fit comfortably in the scooped palms of your hands. From the tip of its nose to the end of its rump, it measures 5 to 8 inches (12–20 cm) in length. The tail, almost 5 inches (12 cm) in length, can be as long as its body.

The endearing appearance of the degu is partly attributable to its large, bright, dark eyes and well-developed, kidney-shaped ears, which give it an impish expression. The large ears are sparsely covered with short hair and set on a rather large head. Long whiskers accentuate the degu's broad face and small nose. The fur on the feet is white or gray. All four feet have four well-developed toes. On the hind feet, the fifth toe is poorly developed, and on the front feet it has only a nail instead of a claw. Stiff, bristlelike hairs extend over the claws of the hind feet.

The fur is soft to the touch and brown to gray-brown in color, with a yellow or orange cast. A paler shade of yellow-brown is noted above and below the eyes and sometimes there is a light band, or collar, around the neck. The belly hair is creamy yellow in color. The tail is dark brown and covered with short hairs at the base. These hairs become longer as they near the end of the tail, where they end in a black tuft.

Anatomy

✔ **Eyes:** Degus have large eyes and excellent eyesight. They depend upon vision to detect and avoid predators, as well as to communicate with one another through body posturing.

✔ **Ears:** Degus rely on their excellent hearing abilities to communicate with one another through voice signals and to listen for approaching danger. Their large ears serve to capture and direct sounds and to dissipate body heat.

✔ **Nose:** Although degus have small noses, their sense of smell (olfaction) is very keen and plays an important part in their social life. Odors and scent-marking are forms of communication used by degus to recognize individual members of their colony.

✔ **Body:** Degus have compact, solid, robust bodies, yet they are agile and able to squeeze into the smallest of spaces in the event of danger.

✔ **Legs and feet:** Degu legs and feet may appear delicate, but they are surprisingly powerful for the animal's small size. A degu can leap several feet high, climb with ease, and run with great speed for long distances when necessary.

✔ **Tail:** Degus signal with their tails as a form of visual communication. The tail is fragile and can easily separate from the body. Extreme care must be taken when handling a degu's tail because the animal can rapidly spin itself around, causing the tail to slip out of its skin, and leaving the bones, flesh, and tendons of the tail exposed. When this occurs there is little bleeding. Once the degu has escaped to a suitable hiding place, it bites off the remaining tail stump. The stump usually heals quickly without complications, but the missing portion of the tail does not grow back. This effective defense mechanism, common among many rodents, permits escape from predators. It also makes handling a degu by the tail a delicate and risky operation. Pets that are frequently handled and

Adult Degu Measurements

Adult	*Weight*	*Length of Head and Body*	*Length of Tail*	*Ear Length*	*Length of Hind Foot*
Male	8 to 14 ounces (250 to 400 g)	10 to 12 inches (250 to 310 mm)	3 to 5 inches (75 to 130 mm)	1.2 inches (30 mm)	1.5 inches (38 mm)
Female	6 to 10.5 ounces (170 g to 300 g)	10 to 12 inches (250 to 300 mm)	3 to 5 inches (75 to 130 mm)	1 inch (25 mm)	1.4 inches (35 mm)

know their owners seldom panic or attempt to escape, but to prevent accidental injury, *it is safest to always scoop a degu up in both hands and to never lift or restrain it by the tail.*

✔ **Teeth:** The degu has many interesting anatomical features, several of which are unique to its species. It has 20 teeth, consisting of four front teeth (incisors) that are pale orange or orange in color (two upper and two lower), and 16 cheek teeth (one premolar and three molars on each side, upper and lower jaws). The premolars are less complex than the molars—a primitive characteristic, according to zoologists. The grinding surface of the cheek teeth resembles a figure-eight shape, giving the family its scientific name, Octodontidae, meaning "eight teeth."

✔ **Special anatomical features:** Like all mammals, degus have one pair of kidneys. Their kidneys are very efficient and allow them to concentrate certain elements in the urine and to conserve other elements in the body.

The nipples on the mammary glands are strategically located, three pair high on the side of the body, between the front and hind limbs, and one pair on the belly between the hind limbs in the inguinal region. This arrangement allows the mother to nurse her offspring in a huddled position, while staying alert to possible predators.

The female degu's uterus is bicornate, meaning the uterus branches into two parts. These two elongated parts of the uterus, called uterine

Degu Dental Formula

i 1/1, c 0/0, p 1/1, *m* 3/3 = 20

The number above the slash represents one-half of the upper jaw (left or right side) and the number under the slash represents one-half of the bottom jaw (left or right side).

i = incisors
c = canine teeth
p = premolars
m = molars

For example, there is one incisor in the upper jaw on the right side and one incisor in the right side of the lower jaw, no canine teeth in the mouth, one premolar in the right side of the upper jaw and one premolar in the right side of the lower. Finally, there are three molars in the right side of the upper jaw and three opposing molars in the right side of the lower jaw for a total of ten teeth. Multiply ten by two, to include all the teeth on the left side of the mouth, and the total number of teeth equals 20.

Degu Facts

Scientific name	Octodon degus
Other names	Trumpet tail, bori, Cuming's octodon, *rata de las cercas, ratón de trompeta*
Origin	Chile
Color	Brown with light cream belly and white feet
Behavior	Good-natured, gentle, active, very sociable
Lifestyle	Live in underground burrows, excellent parents, father helps raise the babies
Life span	5–8 years, possibly longer in captivity

The degu is a South American rodent, native to Chile.

Your degu will spend a lot of time in the highest lookout point it can find in the cage. This is usually the top of the nest box!

Degus have keen senses of sight, hearing, and smell. Those bright eyes and big ears don't miss a thing!

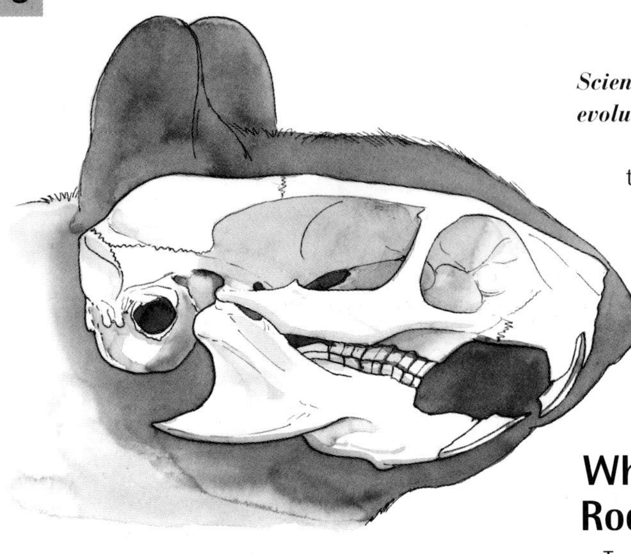

Scientists can tell a lot about degus and their evolution by studying their teeth and skull.

horns, make it easier for the degu to carry and give birth to several young.

Degus have very large adrenal glands compared to other rodents of their size, a double thymus gland, and a genetic makeup of 26 chromosome pairs (58 chromosomes).

✔ **Brain:** The brain of the degu is somewhat unusual for most rodent species. The olfactory bulb is extremely well developed, an indicator that the animal's sense of smell is very keen. Even more interesting is the fact that the brain is moderately convoluted. A direct correlation between intelligence and brain convolution has been suggested in other species. It would seem that the degu is as smart as it looks!

Degu Taxonomy

Kingdom Animalia
Phylum Chordata
Class Mammalia
Order Rodentia
Suborder Hystricognathi
Caviomorpha = South American Hystricomorpha
Family Octodontidae
Genus Octodon
Species degus

What Makes Degus Rodents?

To better understand your degu's personality, habits, instincts, and various requirements, it helps to have an appreciation of just what kind of an animal your degu is. Degus are rodents. Rodents are among the most diverse and numerous of mammalian species. (**Note:** Recently a few popular press articles have suggested that the degu is more closely related to rabbits than rodents, but this is incorrect. Degus are definitely rodents!)

What Are Rodents?

Rodents are remarkably uniform in structural characters. All rodents have four incisors, two upper and two lower. These front teeth grow throughout life, continuously being pushed up from the bottom of the jaw, to compensate for the continual wear they receive from biting hard objects. There are no nerves in the front teeth, except at the base where they grow, and continual wear of the incisors maintains very sharp cutting surfaces. Rodents do not have canine teeth or anterior premolars, so there is a rather large space between the front teeth and

Degu Biology

Natural habitat	Subtropical climate, terrain of shrubs, rocks
Number of chromosomes	58 (29 chromosome pairs)
Natural illness	Diabetes, cataracts
Body temperature	101.8°F (37.9°C)
Ability to concentrate urine	Very efficient kidneys
Sensitivity to high altitudes	Poorly adapted to life at high elevations

the cheek teeth. The cheek teeth are used for grinding and may have many peculiar patterns. These dental patterns, as well as jaw structure, are useful to zoologists and paleontologists for determining how different rodent species developed over time, their relationship to each other, and their origin.

Classification: Rodents are classified according to anatomical characteristics, similarities in teeth and bone structure, origin, and lifestyle. You will sometimes find the degu referred to as being a hystricomorph rodent or a caviomorph rodent. The word "hystricomorph" has both systematic classification and structural meanings. Hystricomorph refers to a particular type of skull and muscle structure seen in certain rodent species, and a very rare type of bottom jaw structure and angulation, called a hystricognathous mandible. The term "caviomorph" literally means "porcupinelike." This classification has nothing to do with porcupine quills, but is based on the similarity of jaw muscles and muscle attachments among rodents in that group. Members of the Caviomorpha taxon are also known as the South American hystricognaths. Although the terminology may seem confusing

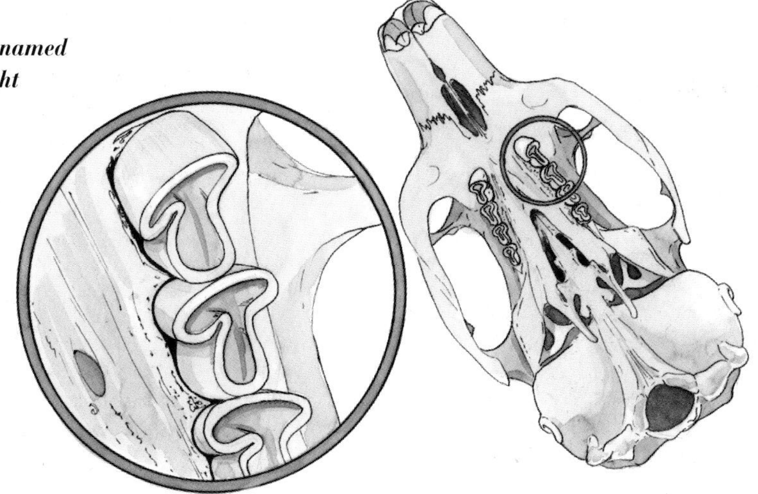

***Octodon degus** is named after the figure eight pattern observed on the surface of the molars.*

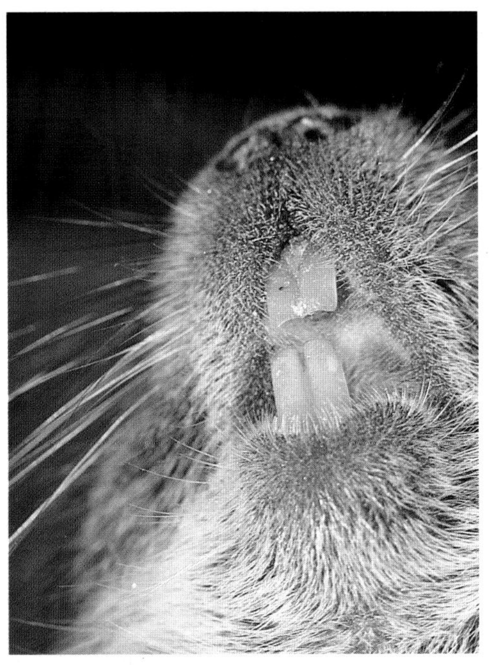

Degus have impressive front teeth! The dark yellow-orange coloration is normal.

at first, the names reflect the origins and evolution of the degu and its ancestors through the ages. For our purposes, the terms hystricomorph and caviomorph can be used interchangeably.

The Degu's Place in Nature

Animals, insects, and plants are classified and grouped according to their differences and similarities. Names are assigned according to kingdom, phylum, class, order, family, genus, and species. With each progressive category, animals grouped together are more closely related. For example, all animals are part of

Degus are extremely sociable animals that live together in colonies.

Degus have distinctive tails that have earned them the nickname, "trumpet tail."

the Kingdom Animalia, but only rodents are members of the Order Rodentia. The name given to a class, order, family, genus, or species may come from different sources. Animals can be named according to a special characteristic of their group, named after the person who discovered them, or even named after the geographical area they naturally inhabit.

Degu Classification

The degu is a member of the Kingdom Animalia (Animal Kingdom), the Phylum Chordata (animals having spinal columns), and the Class Mammalia (mammals). The word *mammalia* refers to the mammary glands (mammae, teats, or breasts). Newborn and baby mammals are nourished by milk from their mothers' breasts. All warm-blooded animals with hair or fur have mammary glands and belong to the Class Mammalia.

Order Rodentia: The word Rodentia is derived from the Latin word *Rodere*, which means "to gnaw." This refers to a rodent's need to constantly chew on hard objects to keep the

Your degu will be a continual source of entertainment for you.

teeth from growing too long. The most important characteristic shared by all rodents is the continual growth of their front teeth throughout their entire lives. Within the Order Rodentia, there are three suborders. The degu belongs to the Suborder Hystricognathi, sometimes called Hystricomorpha (or Caviomorpha).

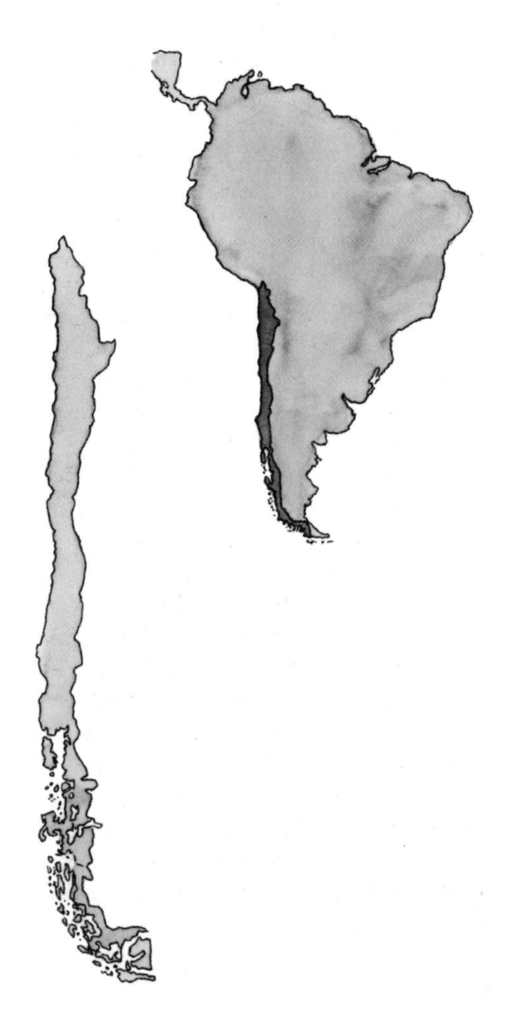

Family: Rodents may be further classified into more closely related groups called families. There are 29 recent rodent families. The degu belongs to a small family called Octodontidae, which holds the dubious distinction of being the most primitive family in the Hystricomorph suborder, according to the fossil record. Loosely translated, Octodontidae means "eight teeth" and refers to the figure-eight, or kidney shape, of the grinding surface of the cheek teeth.

Genus and species: Families are further divided into genera, a collection of even more closely related animals. There are 426 rodent genera. The genus *Octodon* contains only three species, including the degu, whose scientific species name is *degus*.

Common names: The degu has many common, nonscientific names, including the trumpet tail, *chozchoris*, *rata de las cercas*, *ratón de tapias*, *ratón de trompeta*, bori, and Cuming's octodon.

No matter what name you use, the degu remains one of the most interesting, unique, and historically controversial of the 1,814 species of rodents in existence today.

Mysterious History

The early fossil record is incomplete and lively discourse still continues among scientists as to the degu's true origins. It is generally accepted that all South American rodents had a common ancestor somewhere, sometime—but where and when remain a mystery.

Degus come from the southwest slopes of the Andes Mountains in Chile.

Early Ancestors

Many researchers are convinced the degu's ancestors came from North America during the Eocene period (about 55 million years ago), and that they evolved separately from rodents in the Old World that resembled them. They base their idea on specific skull, jaw, and tooth development, which they believe rules out the likelihood of a direct descendant from an African species. They have also found fossils of possible ancestral rodents in Texas and Central America to support their theory.

Other scientists believe the degu's ancestors evolved during the same time period, but from a very primitive African mammal, which itself was derived from partly African and partly Eurasian predecessors. In the middle Eocene to lower Oligocene periods (about 40 million years ago) these animals would have crossed the Atlantic Ocean, presumably on rafts formed from wood, leaves, and debris carried by ocean currents. If the continents were at that time located as close together as the theory of plate tectonics (continental drift) would imply, the cross-Atlantic Ocean voyage millions of years ago would have been shorter than it is today. Nevertheless, at that time in prehistory the trip would still have been approximately 1,800 miles—quite a feat for a group of small ancestral rodents!

Researchers have discovered a worm that parasitizes rodents in both West Africa and South America. This parasite lends support to the raft migration theory, suggesting that when rodents crossed the oceans millions of years ago, they brought their specific parasites with them.

A Rodent Success Story

Although the origin of the degu remains uncertain, we do know that a common ancestor of today's Caviomorph invaded South America after the late Eocene period, and that there is no fossil record of any rodent species existing in South America prior to that time. When rodents reached South America, it appears they had no significant predators. They rapidly adapted, proliferated, and diversified. Rodents filled almost every kind of biological niche they could as they evolved into new and different species. They became such a large and successful group that the small, native South American marsupials could not compete with them. The marsupial became extinct soon after the rodent invasion, while the degu's ancestors went on to become the most dominant species in South America.

Today the degu continues to thrive in the wild and for many years has attracted the interest of scientists around the world. The degu's communal lifestyle, complex behavior, interesting and unusual anatomy, sleep/wake patterns, and various forms of communication are just a few of the many characteristics that have intrigued researchers for decades.

In the mid-1960s, the degu was introduced into the United States and the United Kingdom for use in physiological, medical, and behavioral studies. Twenty adult degus were trapped near Lampa, Chile, in 1964 and sent to the Massachusetts Institute of Technology. The National Zoo later acquired the descendants of these first importations. Eventually the degu made its way into pet stores and into the animal lover's heart.

BEFORE YOU BUY

Just because degus are small doesn't mean there isn't a lot to consider before you can add one to your family. Responsible pet ownership always involves a certain amount of planning, commitment, time, and expense.

Special Considerations

In all fairness to yourself and your future pet, always do your homework first and learn as much as possible about the animal, its requirements, its health, and its behavior. Too often people buy pets on the spur of the moment, when a tiny creature pulls at their heartstrings through the pet-shop window. Although it is tempting, it is unwise to buy any animal on an impulse. "Impulse buyers" have not fully considered all the ramifications of pet ownership. Sadly, people who purchase pets under these conditions often regret their actions when they realize they and their pets are not a good match. Even worse, many of the animals become unwanted. A degu deserves better than that!

Degus are delightful, active animals with a mind and an agenda of their own. They are fascinating to watch, enjoy being held and petted, return affection, and are easy to maintain in captivity. But be careful! They are quick and nimble and can leap high and run very fast. They are difficult to catch if they escape!

Degus are active pets that require plenty of space for housing, toys, and play.

So if you prefer to simply relax and watch these inquisitive creatures at play, that's fine, too. Degus are great entertainers.

What to Consider

So now that you have fallen in love with degus, you want to know whether one of these small animals will be compatible with your lifestyle before introducing one (or preferably more) into your home. The following considerations are offered to help you decide.

Your Lifestyle

You are the first consideration. Who you are, how you live, and what you do are important factors in assessing how well a degu will fit into your lifestyle. The addition of a new pet should be nothing less than a happy and positive experience for you.

It has been well documented that pet ownership has many benefits. People who own animals have been known to derive certain physiological and psychological benefits from the close human–animal bond they form. Pet owners feel wanted, needed, and loved, and indeed they are. After all, their animals depend on them for food and care, and give affection and companionship in return. Caressing or holding an animal has been shown to reduce blood pressure in some cases. Recent medical research suggests that people who own pets may even live longer!

But pet ownership is not always easy. In addition to time and money commitments, there is the sadness that accompanies the eventual, and inevitable, illness, loss, or death of an animal friend. Naturally, the longer you have a pet, the more attached you become to it. Because degus are so affectionate, and because they have longer life spans than most rodent pets, when they are gone they leave behind a tremendous sense of loss.

Some people (such as those with allergies to pet dander or with compromised immune systems) simply cannot have pets, no matter how much they love them.

So consider yourself first. Are you ready for a new pet?

Cost

Contrary to what many people think, the greatest expense of pet ownership is not the purchase price of the animal. Actually, the purchase price is usually insignificant compared to the costs involved in time, housing, feed, space, toys, and veterinary care.

The price of a degu will vary with supply and demand, the animal's age, tameness, and how easy it is to handle. Degus are usually more expensive than more common rodent pocket pets. For example, they may easily cost five times the price of a pet rat. This is due in part to their relatively long gestation period, their limited availability in many areas, and their increasing popularity.

Time

Fortunately, degus are not demanding pets and they do not require a great deal of time. The number of degus you own and the size of their cage will determine how often you will need to clean the cage (see Accommodations for Your Degu). Most cages do not need to be cleaned more than once a week. Fresh water and food must be provided daily (see Feeding Your Degu). Be sure to take a few minutes each day to handle your degu. This contact is important to keep your degu tame and maintain its bond of affection for you. Degus enjoy interacting with their owners and can become lonely if they are ignored for too long. While you are holding or caressing your degu, check it over thoroughly to be sure it is healthy and doing well. Simply observe your pet for normal appearance and behavior. Visiting, handling, feeding, and watering take only a few minutes a day—a small investment to ensure that your bright-eyed companion is healthy and content.

Materials

Degus do require a few basic essentials: safe, comfortable, escape-proof housing with a secure door or lid; nutritious food; appropriate bedding material; a water bottle or dish; a nest box or hiding place; and chew toys.

Exercise wheels: Your degu especially needs plenty of exercise. This is easy to provide in the form of an exercise wheel. An exercise wheel is not only a toy—it is a necessity. Degus have been known to run miles in an evening simply by working out in their wheels. Ideally, the exercise wheel you purchase should have a solid floor, rather than rungs. This will prevent your pet from accidentally being caught and injured between the rungs of the wheel or from developing sores on its feet, sometimes called "bumblefoot." The exercise wheel should be large, at least 10 to 12 inches (25–30 cm) in diameter and 4 inches (10 cm) wide. This is because degus like to really stretch out when they run and because they will often run in the wheel together at the same time. If you have several animals housed together, you might want to consider buying an additional exercise wheel. Two large exercise wheels require a lot of cage space, which means you will need space in your home for a fairly large cage.

Playthings: Degus enjoy any toys or activities that make life more interesting. Favorite degu playthings include chew sticks, hamster running balls, dust baths, ladders and ramps to climb, and tubes and tunnels. You can make many degu toys yourself, such as inexpensive tunnels from PVC plumbing pipe from your local hardware store, or wooden nest boxes and hiding places from untreated, nontoxic wood, and branches from nonpoisonous plants and trees for them to climb.

Space

Your degu requires more cage space than most rodents. This is because degus like to jump, leap, climb, and run fast, and all of these activities require extra space. Of course, the more degus you house together, the greater the cage space they will require.

Location: Finding just the right location for your pet's cage is important. It must be out of direct sunlight, especially if part of the cage is made of glass or Plexiglas. Even if the temperature within your home is comfortable, a solid-walled cage placed in direct sunlight can heat up rapidly, just like a greenhouse. The inside of the cage can become extremely hot and your degu could die from heatstroke. It is also important to place the cage in an area away from cold and drafts so your degu does not become chilled and develop pneumonia. This is especially important to protect the health of baby degus.

Finally, try to place your degu's housing at a comfortable level for viewing and handling. Ideally you will want to find a location where you can enjoy your pet's activities and be able to reach in to catch it or feed it, clean the cage, change the water bottle, and replace the bedding without having to bend over or stoop.

Other Household Pets

One of the biggest threats to a degu is the presence of another animal. Degus have a very keen sense of smell. They know when there are other animals in the house. Your degu can

Do not allow other household pets near your degu where they can harm it.

Are you ready to add a degu to your family?

Degus love to climb. Be sure the branches you provide your pet are from nontoxic plants and safe to chew.

become stressed or frightened if your other pets come near its cage. Make sure the lid or door to your degu's cage is securely fastened. Be sure to place the cage well out of reach of the family dog, cat, ferret, bird, or any other pet. You probably never thought of your house pets as being harmful, but cats and ferrets are natural hunters and dogs can play rough. Even birds can quickly peck a small rodent to death. And large pet reptiles would find your degu to be the ideal size for a meal. Although a degu can inflict serious bite wounds when frightened, it is mild-mannered and nonaggressive. It is certainly no match for these animals. For the safety of all the pets in your household, keep your degu well isolated.

Children

For everyone's viewing enjoyment you will want to place your degu's cage where its activities can be easily observed. Inquisitive small children are naturally drawn to animals and interesting cages and containers. Unfortunately small children can also accidentally drop the animal (leading to possible injury, escape, or loss) or try to restrain it by the tail (causing the tail to come off). For these reasons, children should be supervised at all times while watching or handling the degu. To prevent injury to your pet, and heartbreak to the child, be sure to teach children in the household how to correctly and gently pick up and handle a degu. It is safest if very young children only observe the animal, or pet it while it is in its cage or while an adult holds it for them. Depending on how tame your degu is, older children may be able to sit down and hold it with both hands. Degus know and recognize their owners. Your degu may be calm around you and easy for you to handle, but a stranger's voice, or a child's sudden movements, may startle it. And if your degu is frightened, it may bite or try to escape. It takes only a split second for your degu to slip out of small hands, but it may require hours to capture it, assuming you are lucky enough to do so. The safety of the child and the degu is your responsibility. When you cannot be there to supervise their activity, place the degu cage out of the reach of small children. This is a safety measure well worth the temporary inconvenience.

Crepuscular Activities

Degus are busy during the day and night. Their normal activity is called "crepuscular," in reference to their peaks of activity during dusk and dawn, with intermittent sleep and wakefulness at other times of the day. (The word "crepuscular" comes from the French word, "crépuscule," which means "twilight.") Although considered to be a diurnal species (most active during the daytime), recent information collected by experts in sleep research at Stanford University indicates the degu experiences highly fragmented sleep-wake patterns. They take "catnaps" throughout the day. In addition, their day and night activity levels can be influenced by outside factors. For example, if your degu has unlimited access to an exercise wheel, it will become more active during the night (nocturnal). In this case, if you are a light sleeper, you will want to place your degu's cage somewhere in your home where the sounds of your pet in the running wheel will not disturb you. Or, you may decide to give your degu access to its exercise wheel during the daytime only. Your degu will then be more active during the day and you can both sleep well at night.

Veterinary Care

Degus are generally hardy animals that do very well with good care and nutrition. However, if your pet becomes sick or injured, you may need to take it to your veterinarian for an examination and possible treatment. If you own several degus, and one of them is sick, it is important to determine the cause of illness to be sure that the problem is not contagious to your other pets.

Many veterinarians specialize in pocket pets, or have a special interest in these small animals. Pocket pets have nutritional, housing, and

An exercise wheel is more than a toy. It is a necessity to keep your pet in good physical condition.

If your pet doesn't seem to be itself, contact a veterinarian who has a special interest in pocket pets.

medical requirements that are very different from the larger companion animals. They can be sensitive to certain products and medications used for treating more common pets.

It is a good idea to contact veterinarians in advance of needing veterinary care. This gives you an opportunity to introduce yourself as a possible future client and meet the veterinarians in your area who have an expertise in pocket pets. You can then decide beforehand where you would like to take your degu if it becomes ill, and not be burdened with this decision during a possible emergency situation.

When to Acquire a New Pet

Although you may want a degu right now, today might not be the best time to buy your pet. With the degu's growing popularity, the demand for degus has also increased and sometimes the supply cannot fill the demand. Breeders and pet shops may ask you to place a special order to reserve your pet, especially if you are looking for a recently weaned baby degu. Sometimes it's hard to be patient, but in the end it's worth the wait. By buying a degu of the age, sex, and temperament you want, you won't be disappointed.

If you have several obligations and your free time is limited, you may want to postpone buying your degu until you will have more time to enjoy it. For example, if you are moving or changing jobs, a new pet may be added stress rather than enjoyment. If you are planning a vacation soon, you will have to make arrangements for animal care in your absence.

Some animals are purchased during the holidays as gifts for someone else. This brings up three very important points.

1. Although it is tempting, it is never a good idea to buy a pet as a gift. Pet ownership is a responsibility that someone else may not want to assume.

2. Adding a new pet to the family during the holiday season should be discouraged. This is a time when most people already have plenty to do with visitors, deadlines, and commitments. A new pet can be overlooked in the busy shuffle with all the distractions and excitement. Families do not have time to learn about, observe, socialize, and care for a new pet during the holidays. Visitors and guests unfamiliar with proper handling techniques may stress and frighten the new degu and be bitten, or mishandle the animal, causing it to lose its tail (see HOW-TO: Handling). Someone may forget to close the cage door or lid. Holidays are a time when many pets escape from home and degus are good escape artists and difficult to catch.

3. Pets bought during the holidays may be more stressed or prone to illness than usual. With the greater demand for pets during this time, animals may be separated from their mothers and weaned too early, or shipped long distances in cold weather. These stressful situations can lead to illness and even death. There are, of course, animal protection laws, but it is good to be aware of potential problems.

Selecting Your Degu

Where to Find a Degu

Degus may be purchased from degu breeders and hobbyists advertising in pet magazines (available in bookstores and pet shops), local newspapers, or on the Internet. They may also be found in pet stores (listed in your telephone book). Your veterinarian may also know some degu breeders you can contact.

How to Select Your Degu

If possible, visit as many degu breeders and pet stores as possible and look at as many degus as you can before you make a selection. This way you can compare the overall health and quality of the animals, the cleanliness of their environment, their sociability, and the different price ranges.

Once you have chosen a degu to take home, ask if you can pick it up and hold it before you buy it. You will quickly learn how tame the degu is by how well it behaves when you handle it. If it squeaks, squeals, or tries to bite, you probably want to continue your search for a less frightened and more socialized individual!

If the degu you have selected is tame and allows you to handle it gently, examine it closely to be sure it is in good health. Are the eyes bright and clear? Is the coat shiny and does the skin look healthy and free of parasites? If possible, examine the front teeth to make sure they are properly aligned in the mouth. The teeth should be a dark yellow-orange color. White teeth are not normal for degus and often indicate poor health or a dietary deficiency.

The degu(s) you finally select will depend on availability, their physical attributes, and your personal preferences. Of all the animals you have visited, which ones appeal most to you? Which are the most healthy, friendly, and playful? Which ones have the most personality? The hardest thing about choosing a degu to join your family is leaving the other ones behind!

How Many Degus to Keep

If you simply want an interesting companion in your home, one degu can certainly fill the bill. Degus are capable of providing a lot of company. However, in all fairness to your pet, remember that degus are very sociable animals that can become very lonely. They are communal animals that thrive on interactions with members of their own species. They enjoy cuddling up with a companion in the nest box or running tandem in the exercise wheel. For these reasons, it is highly recommended that you keep a minimum of two degus (ideally a male and a female, or two compatible females), especially if your schedule requires long or frequent absences. Keeping more than one degu is a

Although it is tempting, never buy a pet as a gift for someone else. Holidays are an especially impractical time to add a pet to the family. Wait until you have the time you need to learn about and care for your pet.

good thing for you, too. It is always a comfort to have a degu to cheer you up if one of the others should die.

If you are thinking about raising degus as a hobby, you will need to buy at least one pair of degus. In this case, you will want to find one or more reputable degu breeders. An experienced degu breeder can be a valuable source of information and answer many questions about degu behavior and resources. They may even have information about rodent or pocket pet clubs in your area. Clubs are a great way to meet other people who share your interests in these fascinating animals.

How many degus you own is purely up to you. Degus should be fun. You never want to have so many animals that it seems you spend more time cleaning up after them than enjoying them. Keep your animal numbers reasonable so most of the time you spend with your degus will be fun time! The number of degus you keep all depends on your lifestyle, how much housing space you can provide, and the amount of time you can dedicate to cultivating your friendship with these charming creatures.

Male or Female

The decision whether to acquire a male or a female degu will depend on your reasons for buying a degu. If you are simply looking for a great pet and an interesting companion, you will be happy with either a male or female degu. If you are planning to raise degus, you will obviously need at least one pair to begin your project.

Your pet will look forward to your visits. Regular handling will make it tame and well-mannered.

Degus are very social. If possible, always house at least two together.

Degus don't grow on trees! They are cute but not always easy to find. It may take time to locate a degu supplier or you may have to wait a while until some are available.

Physical differences: The main physical difference you will note is that the male degu is slightly larger than the nonpregnant female. Otherwise, the anatomical differences are subtle. Unlike many rodents, the male's testicles are retained in the abdomen so there is no visible scrotum. The main behavioral differences will be the male's tendency to urinate more frequently, as a way of scent-marking his territory (see Understanding Your Degu). Don't worry. Although other animals can detect your degu's scent, you pet will be virtually odorless to you as long as you keep the cage and bedding clean.

Age and Longevity

The ideal age to bring your new degu home is when it is recently weaned and no longer needs its mother for nutrition, warmth, and protection. There are two good reasons to buy a young degu rather than an older one. First, a baby degu is gentler and easier to handle and tame. A baby will adapt quickly to you and its new home. Second, degus have long life spans. The sooner you acquire your degu, the sooner you can socialize it and integrate it into your family and the easier it is for the baby to bond with you. An older animal has a more difficult time adapting to a change in surroundings or

Young children should always have adult supervision when they play with a degu.

lifestyle. And of course, the earlier you obtain your pet, the more time you will have to share with it and enjoy it.

How long do degus live? The life span will vary with each individual animal and the care and nutrition it receives. On average, degus can live five to nine years, representing a long-term ownership commitment on your part. During this time you will no doubt develop a strong emotional attachment to your endearing pet and when it dies you will experience the heartache that accompanies such a loss. If you already know you want degus to be part of your life for several years, keep at least two or more degus at a time. Having more than one degu will help ease the pain and fill the void when one of the other degus eventually dies.

Children and Degus

Degus make interesting and educational pets for children. Very young children must learn, however, that it is safer to observe degus in their cages rather than attempt to hold them because they can escape so easily.

Important Lessons

The first thing children should learn about any pet is not to put their face up close against the animal. It is very tempting to rub a cheek across the soft fur, or even try to kiss the animal. But be sure to teach children from the very beginning that this is the one thing they must not do. The majority of all animal bite wounds inflicted on children (regardless of animal species) happen in the area of the face and head.

With adult guidance, there is no limit to the things children can learn from a pet degu. Degu ownership provides an excellent opportunity for adults to teach children about pets, the importance of humane care and treatment, and respect for life. Children can learn about the degu's evolutionary history, its activities, play behavior, favorite foods, and even its reproduction. It is amazing to watch how dedicated degu parents are while they raise their family.

A degu in the house is a great way for very young children to learn to be responsible. They can participate in the degu's care and learn about the importance of fresh water, good food, and a clean home. Older children can learn a lot about animal behavior and biology, simply by observing the degu's many activities. Degus can make wonderful school science projects. They can be the focus of study for topics such as animal behavior, exercise, or reproduction.

Some children are uncomfortable around animals, especially large animals. Because a degu is small, it can make it possible for a child to replace anxiety, fear, or timidity with tenderness and affection. Adult supervision is necessary when a child is handling a degu. Supervision prevents accidental bite injuries to the child and accidental escape or injury to the degu.

Even children who are somewhat shy will often talk freely when they are in the presence of animals. A degu can open doors of communication and learning for a child. While sitting still and observing such a fascinating animal, a child becomes a captive audience and a good learner. Together you and a child can share thoughts and ideas about animals, people, families, and anything else you can relate to degus and humans on the child's level.

Animal Life and Death

Even with the best possible care, degus eventually become ill or die. Because degus have a relatively long life span, they require a long-term commitment from you, not a child. Make sure that you share as much, or more, interest in the degu as the child does. Remember that children's interests naturally change. It would be unreasonable not to expect a child's interest in degus to eventually dwindle over time. So be prepared for that possible day when you might be solely responsible for the degu's care. On the other hand, a child can be quite enamored with a small rodent friend and remain attentive to the animal for years.

A Child's First Loss

Children are very sensitive to issues of animal life and death. The death of a pet degu may be the first loss a child experiences. It is very important that the child is prepared in advance for the eventual, and inevitable, loss or death of a beloved pet. It is especially important that this preparation be provided in a compassionate manner appropriate for the child's age and level of maturity. The loss of a pet can be a very emotional experience for a child. But if handled skillfully, this loss can be turned into a positive learning experience. It provides an opportunity in which you may openly discuss life, love, illness, or death and possibly address additional fears or concerns the child may have. A small degu can play a big part in helping a child grow, mature, and strengthen in character.

UNDERSTANDING YOUR DEGU

The degu's success as a species and its ability to survive in the wild are due in large part to its highly social lifestyle. Social relations are important to degu community living, which is why degus have developed complex behaviors and various forms of communication.

A degu must be able to recognize and identify other members of its colony and extended family group and interact with each individual in an appropriate manner. Degus communicate in many ways:

✔ voice signals, or vocalizations
✔ sense of touch, or tactile communication
✔ sense of smell and olfactory signals
✔ body language, or visual communication

Here are some basic degu behaviors to help you learn how to interpret your degu's moods and attitudes.

The Basics

Communication and Behavior

"If only my pet could talk, what would it tell me?" Ever since humans have kept pets, they have wondered what their animals would say to them if they could speak. But the old saying, "actions speak louder than words," holds true for degus as well as people. Degus are very expressive animals. Once you learn your degu's "language" of sounds, scents, and body postures, you will see why degus have no need for words.

Degus are expert communicators.

For example, you will easily recognize the times your degu feels comfortable and secure. Its sense of well-being is contagious as it literally frolics in its cage, runs in its exercise wheel, grooms itself and its companions, climbs, jumps, explores, and snacks on favorite foods. All of these activities are signs of a happy, healthy degu.

However, there is more to degu behavior than one might think. Degus have many behavioral characteristics that are unusual for rodents. For example, courtship rituals are rare in mammalian species in general, yet degus exhibit distinct courtship behavior patterns (see Raising Degus). In addition, to increase the chances of survival of their babies, mother degus have adapted their parenting styles according to the habitat in which they live and father degus are extremely attentive and

Male degus are very dedicated and protective parents.

protective of their young. In fact, all the degus in the colony do their best to make sure the babies do well. If the father degu is unavailable to help, or if the mother degu simply needs assistance, other females degus will often take turns being "nannies" and babysitting the babies. If the parents should die, other degus in the colony will adopt the babies and integrate them into their own families.

As you observe your degu on a daily basis, you will appreciate the fact that almost everything your degu does, it does for a good reason. Its behavior and communication reflect millions of years of ancestral development that make it possible for the degu, one of the most primitive of rodent species, to survive to the present day.

Body Language (Visual Cues)

Degus necessarily have excellent vision to help them identify other animals and avoid predators. A large part of degu communication is accomplished by sight. They observe and respond to each other through body language, a method of expressing moods and intentions by posturing.

Tail wagging: Degus hold their tails high when they run or are excited. They also signal by thumping their tails on the ground. If you see your degu wagging its tail, or moving its tail up and down, it means that your degu is in an excited state. Tail wagging in degus does not necessarily indicate happiness or pleasure. Rather, tail wagging means your degu is alert. It may be happy or it may feel tense or threatened, depending on the situation. For example, tail wagging is observed when two male degus meet each other and feel uncomfortable about the encounter. Tail wagging, and some body trembling, may occur before or after a fight or confrontation and may indicate aggression or submission, depending upon the animal.

In a totally different setting, that of a male and female encounter, tail wagging by the male can be an act of submission. By wagging his tail, the male is showing that he is aroused, yet remaining submissive until the female will permit him to approach, make contact with her, and investigate whether or not she will accept him for breeding.

Tail up and rump display: When a degu feels threatened it may turn its rump to its opponent and raise its tail. This appears to be another form of submissive behavior. By displaying its hindquarters, the degu hopes to ward off an attack. Rump displays may occur between two male degus, or a male and a female degu. It usually precedes or follows an aggressive action or attack. Often, the opponent will mount the animal that displays its

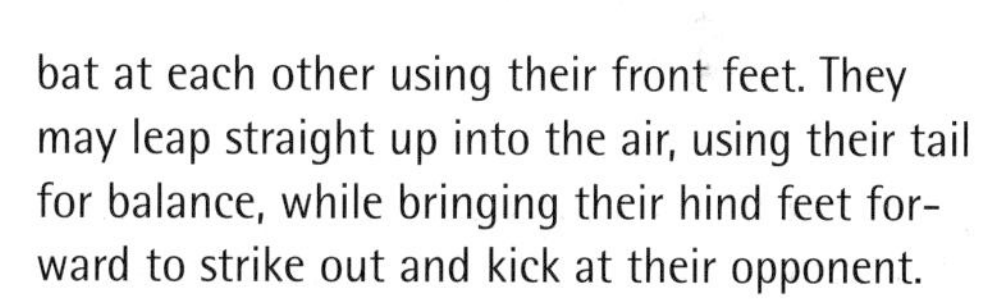

Degus actively protect their territory and family.

rump. This is the aggressor's way of establishing its dominance.

Raised hairs (pilo-erection): Normally a degu's fur lies flat against its body. However, when a degu is planning to attack another animal or if it is startled, it can raise its hair up from its skin. This is called pilo-erection. By making its hair stand up a little higher the degu may be able to fool its opponent into thinking it is larger than it really is and possibly ward off an attack.

Aggressive behavior: Although degus are usually mild-mannered and friendly, there are times when they will fight among themselves. Arguments are usually between male degus in an effort to establish dominance or to protect territory, food, or family. The two males will stand on their hind legs facing one another and bat at each other using their front feet. They may leap straight up into the air, using their tail for balance, while bringing their hind feet forward to strike out and kick at their opponent.

Play behavior: Sometimes you will observe your degu run through an entire repertoire of play behavior consisting of jumps, head tossing, pivots, running, and body twisting. This behavior is especially common in very young degus and is an important form of "antipredator

Degu Body Language

	Situation	*Meaning*	*Function*
Hair-raising (pilo-erection)	Alarmed, encounter with another animal.	Threat.	Frighten opponent, appear larger, intimidate.
Tail wagging	Alert, aroused, courting.	Threat, caution, or submissive behavior.	Allows male to approach female.
Tail rump display	Encounter with aggressive opponent.	Defensive, submissive posture.	Deflect an attack.
	Female encounter with male.	Sexual behavior	Permit breeding.
Hops, jumps, body twisting, running	Play behavior.	Friendly, social interactions, primarily among family (littermates).	Practice movements necessary to escape predators such as hawks and owls.

Degus use a wide range of sounds to communicate with one another. They are constantly alert to each other's calls.

Immediately after breeding, the male degu will guard the female from other male degus and make a repetitive squeaking call that can last for several minutes.

flight" play. It provides a way for degus to practice movements that would allow them to escape from predators. Researchers believe this type of play behavior is stimulated by various odors as it often occurs after sniffing another degu. It is not unusual to see a young degu sniff a littermate then shake its head and leap into the air.

Some forms of play behavior resemble aggressive behavior. This type of play makes it possible for the young degus to practice movements and postures that they will use as adults when they need to claim their territory and establish dominance among other degus.

Play behavior is seen frequently among littermates and young degus. In fact, it is almost exclusively family oriented. It is interesting that littermates are very playful with one another. While the babies play, the father will often stand guard or groom the mother. The mother degu takes her maternal responsibilities very seriously. Her play behavior is limited to sniffing noses with her babies, nuzzling them on the nape of the neck, and allowing them to climb on her back. The father degu provides extensive parental care by huddling and grooming the babies, but he rarely actually plays with the babies. Father degus are extremely dedicated to their family. In captivity, it is possible to pair a male degu with a pregnant female that was bred by a different male. When the baby degus are born, the male degu will guard, protect, and care for them as though they were his own.

Dust baths are used to remove excess oil from the coat and to enable animals in a colony to identify one another by sharing the same odor.

Curiosity and interest: When your degu is curious or interested in something, it will sit up on its haunches and sniff the air, or it will remain on all fours, testing the air and poised to take off at a run at the least disturbance.

Fear: It is easy to tell when your degu is startled. If it can, it will run back to its nest box or hiding place immediately. If your degu is very frightened, it may freeze and remain in place with its ears flattened against its head. This is an excellent defense mechanism in the wild, where the degu's brown color serves as a camouflage among the dirt, shrubs, and rocks of its natural environment. If the degu makes no movement, it has a good chance of avoiding detection by predators.

Degus are gentle animals. A frightened degu is seldom aggressive and rarely attacks. However, if your degu is startled, allow it time to calm down before you try to pick it up because in its fear it may try to bite you when you handle it.

Tactile and Olfactory (Senses of Touch and Smell)

Contact and grooming: One of the most important means of communication among degus is accomplished through sense of touch. When two degus meet for the first time, and if the encounter is not an aggressive one, they usually begin their introductions by making nose-to-nose contact. If there are no objections, the animals become more familiar by sniffing and nuzzling each other's neck, rump, and eventually, perineum. They then proceed to nuzzling and nibbling on each other's mouth and chin and usually conclude with a long grooming session. Degus may groom each other for 10 to 15 minutes at a time. Grooming one another is an important way degus establish amiable relationships in the colony.

Play behavior in degus often begins by sniffing noses with each other.

Huddling: Huddling is a one of the most important aspects of degu life, health, safety, and well-being. Degus love to huddle. By huddling together in a nest or burrow, degus that have established friendly relationships with each other keep warm and share the same body scents. They also share the responsibilities of looking out for danger. When they huddle, degus usually line up alternating nose to rump, side by side. This arrangement allows them to look in opposite directions for warning signs of approaching predators. Huddling is such an integral part of degu behavior and survival that even baby degus huddle in alternating formation in the nest.

Snuggling: It is a sad degu indeed that does not have a snuggling partner. Lone degus are often sad and depressed. If you own more than one degu, when you peek inside the nest box you will notice that no matter how spacious the box is, your degus are crammed as closely together as they can be. You will also see that one degu often tucks its head under the chin of another degu. This close body contact is considered by some scientists to serve as an exchange of olfactory information and individual identification. It is also likely that the animals derive comfort and a sense of security simply from having a companion.

Adult Degu Vocalizations

	Alarm call	*Warning*	*Threat*	*Pain*	*Call to young*	*Greeting or social call*	*Grooming*	*Courting*
Tooth chatter	X	X	X					
Squeak	X	X					X	
Growl			X					
Squeal				X				
Chirp						X		X
Chuckle					X		X	
Chuck-wee						X		
Cluck						X	X	
Gurgle						X	X	
Whimpers						X		

Baby Degu Vocalizations

	Abandonment	Suckling	Grooming
Gurgles			X
Peeps		X	
Squeaks			X
Whistles		X	
Isolation cry	X		
Tooth chatter	X		

Dust bathing: Taking a dust bath is not just a way to keep the fur clean. Degus take dust baths so that they can be socially acceptable by having the same odor. They accomplish this by urinating in the community dusting spot and rolling in it. Urine contains several substances that degus use as a form of communication. Through chemical signals, degus can tell a lot about each other, including their identification. Female degus use chemical signals in their urine to indicate when they are in estrus. In the wild, when a degu plans to invade another's territory, it often rolls in the dusting spot shared by the animals that live in that community. Scientists consider this behavior to be a form of olfactory disguise. Rolling in the dusting area gives the invading degu the same scent as the animals that live in the territory to be invaded. Having the same odor makes it possible for the foreign degu to investigate new territory without being identified as an intruder. If the degu is accepted in the colony, there will be less chance of attack and rejection.

Scent marking: Urine is used extensively as a form of communication among degus. Degus mark their territory by leaving little drops of urine in the area. Male degus scent-mark more frequently than females. During courtship rituals male degus will throw one or both hind limbs over the back of the female and spray urine. This behavior is called enurination and appears to be the male's way of claiming the female as his mate. Courted females will also raise a hind limb over the male and urinate (see Raising Degus).

Auditory (Sense of Hearing)

Vocalization (voice signals): Degus produce a variety of sounds that signal their moods. Researchers have measured, recorded, and categorized the sounds according to duration and frequency. The following is a description of a

A dust bath is a special treat for degus. It is also a social necessity.

few of the sounds you will learn to recognize when your degu decides to express itself through vocalization.

Alarm or warning call: Adult degus in the wild often take positions atop rocks where they can stand sentry duty. If they see any signs of danger, they stand upright and emit a sharp warning squeak to alert the other degus in the colony. Upon hearing the alarm call, degus race to the safety of their burrows.

The same warning call can be heard in captivity. The father degu often stands guard with his head poked out of the nest box, making his warning call at the least disturbance. He will also sit on top of the nest box for a better view of his surroundings. A female will also let out a warning squeak when a male approaches her.

Protest squeak: This squeak sounds much like the alarm call, except that it is longer in duration. The protest squeak is the sound a degu makes when it is uncomfortable or hurt or when another degu grooms it too roughly.

Squeal: The squeal is a long, loud,

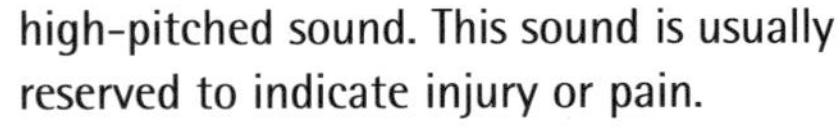

high-pitched sound. This sound is usually reserved to indicate injury or pain.

Protest growl: The protest growl is easy to recognize as a deeper, more guttural sound, similar to a dog or cat growl. It usually precedes an attack on another animal and is often accompanied by tooth chattering. A degu will also growl if it is cornered or feels threatened.

Tooth chatter: Degus that chatter their teeth are frightened, agitated, or angry and may bite or fight. They should be approached with caution and not handled until they have had time to calm down.

Baby degus chatter when they are alone and feel abandoned.

Clucks: The degu's cluck sounds like a cross between a soft chicken cluck and the sound you make when you place your tongue against the roof of your mouth and cluck. Degus cluck, squeak, and gurgle when they groom each other.

Chuck-wee: This special call is a sound degus make when they are alert but not frightened. It sounds like a garbled cluck that ends in a chuckle or buzzing sound. Once your degu has learned to recognize you and looks forward to your visits, this is the call it may use to greet you. Young degus have a special chirping call that may be the equivalent to the adult's chuck-wee call.

Gurgles: When baby degus interact with their littermates and parents, they often gurgle. This sound can best be described as a soft, bubbling sound,

These newborn degus, when left alone, will let out an abandonment call or isolation cry to let their parents know they are distressed.

Degu parents can hear their babies' distress calls from far away and respond immediately.

sometimes with a barely perceptible whistle, almost like the sound you hear just as water starts to boil in a kettle that is about to whistle. Adult degus also gurgle when they interact socially. Gurgles and chuckles often occur together in degu conversations.

Chuckles: Adult degus and their babies make sounds that can best be described as a low chuckling noise. This vocalization is used by adult degus to call to their young. Baby degus chuckle and gurgle when they are being groomed.

Chirps: If you have more than one degu you will sometimes hear them making soft noises that can only be described as sounding like a group of little birds talking softly. These chirps seem to be one way the animals express their contentment when they are together. Degus also chirp to each other when they are courting.

Peeps and whistles: Baby degus make high-pitched peeps and whistles while they are snuggling with their mother and suckling. This sound wakes up sleeping littermates and stimulates them to eat as well.

Whimpers: These sounds are very similar to a puppy dog crying. It seems to be a very social call, used as a greeting or a way to keep track of one another's location by whimpering back and forth to each other.

Abandonment call or isolation cry: When baby degus are left alone in their nest or feel abandoned upon leaving the nest, they will call to their parents in an unmistakable, high-pitched cry. This effective method of letting their parents know they are distressed and insecure draws an instant response. The parents will immediately return to the nest to check on the safety of their babies, or if the baby degus have wandered from the nest, the parents will retrieve them by carrying them home in their mouths.

Post-copulatory squeaks: Immediately after breeding, male degus make a continual squeaking sound, called a post-copulatory squeak. This sounds much like an alarm call and is repeated at intervals of one to three seconds for 5 to 15 minutes or sometimes longer. It is believed that by making this repetitious post-breeding call, the male degu informs competing males of the mating act and prevents them from approaching or attempting to breed the same female. It is important that the male keep competitors at a distance so that the future litter he helps the female raise is in fact his own offspring.

The post-copulatory squeak is unmistakable due to its high pitch and repetitive nature. If you hear this call among your degus, you should mark your calendar and expect to have a litter of little ones in three months!

HOW-TO: HANDLING

Now that you understand degu behavior, body language, and voice signals, you are ready to enjoy handling your pet. Here are some safe ways to pick up your degu.

The Two-handed Technique

This method is the preferred method for handling degus. Place both hands together to form a cup and slowly lower your hands into the cage. Use your hands like a scoop to slide underneath the animal and lift it out of the cage. You may prefer to slide one hand under your pet and cup your other hand on top of it. Be sure to keep your hands cupped tightly so your degu doesn't leap out and fall.

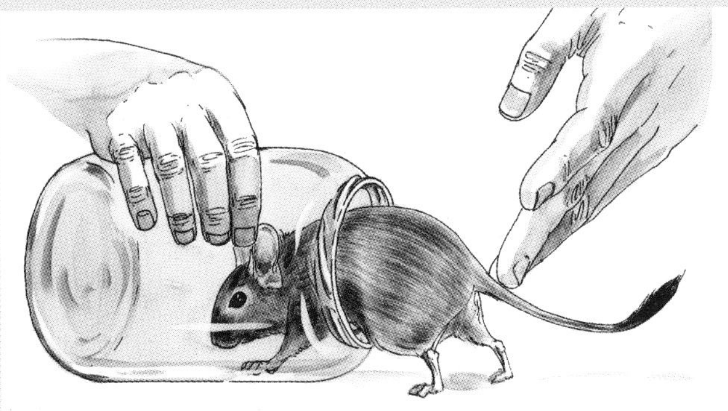

For the inexperienced handler, or for a degu that is difficult to handle, the jar technique is the safest method to use.

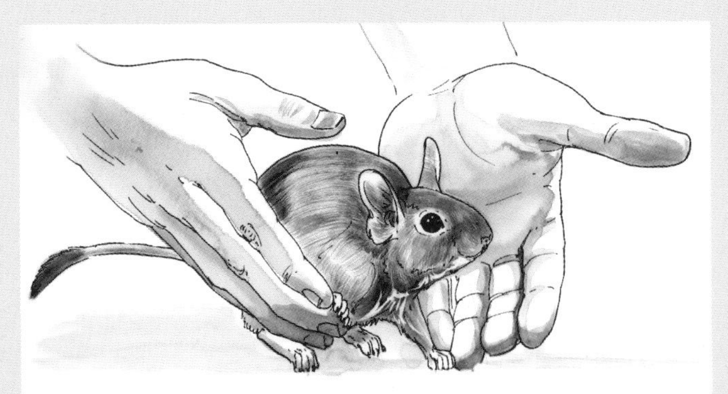

When you use both hands to scoop your degu out of its cage, be sure to approach slowly so your degu sees you and is not startled. A tame degu will often place its feet on your fingers, then willingly climb into your palms.

The Jar Technique

This method is a good one for children who are learning to handle a degu for the first time. A large jar is slowly lowered into the cage and placed in front of the animal so that it is facing the inside of the container. If your degu needs some encouragement, simply hold the jar in one hand and use your other hand to gently push its rump forward so it enters the jar. Be sure to keep the top of the can or jar covered because your degu will try to jump out while you are transporting it.

The One-handed Technique

This technique works for the more skilled handler, working with a very tame degu. One hand is slowly lowered into the cage above the degu's back and the degu is grasped around its middle with the thumb, little finger, and ring finger. Normally, the fingers are pointed in the direction of the animal's head. However, if the fingers are directed toward the degu's rump there is less possibility of being bitten. Hold onto the degu firmly, but not too tightly, while gently lifting it from the cage. A tame degu that knows its handler and feels secure will seldom attempt to bite or struggle to free itself. However, this technique may be difficult or awkward for someone who has large hands.

Net Technique

Sometimes an animal escapes or is frightened or difficult to handle. If you need to catch a degu under these circumstances, a butterfly net or closely woven fish net is ideal. You may want to keep two nets on hand: one with a short handle for use in the cage and one with a long handle to facilitate trapping escaped degus under the furniture.

Gloves

Some people try to use thick gloves when handling small animals. This method is discouraged for several reasons. It is usually unnecessary and cumbersome and degus can easily escape. Using gloves sometimes gives a person a false sense of security, because a degu can still bite through thick gloves. Because it is difficult to restrain a degu with thick gloves, there is a tendency to hold on too tightly, making it hard for the animal to breathe.

✔ Never pick up a degu by its tail.

✔ Never try to pick up a degu by the skin on its neck or back.

Never pick up a degu by the nape of the neck or by the tail.

✔ Forceps, tweezers, or other instruments should never be used to grasp degus.

The best way to enjoy your degu is to handle it carefully and gently every day so that it will remain tame. By using gentle, firm, and safe handling techniques, you will be able to fully enjoy holding and caressing your pet.

ACCOMMODATIONS FOR YOUR DEGU

In their native South America, degus are common, hardy, resilient rodents and have been so for a long time. Charles Darwin reported sighting hundreds of degus during his explorations in the 1800s.

Natural Habitat

Today, with populations often exceeding 150 animals per acre and an appreciation for a vegetarian diet, the degu has become an agricultural pest in many areas of central Chile.

Degus are found in Chile, between the coastal regions and mountain foothills, in areas covered with shrubs, thickets, and rocks. They dig elaborate burrows and chambers for their homes. The openings to the burrows are covered with sticks, small rocks, and cow dung, and mounds of pebbles and sticks are constructed at the burrow entrances as a way of stating ownership and territoriality. Some of the chambers are used for storing food in the winter, although degus do not hibernate. Other chambers are shared by mother degus and their offspring. Interestingly, degus also share their burrows with the chinchilla rat, *Abrocoma bennetti*. The chinchilla rat is a nocturnal rodent about the same size as a degu. It shares a similar lifestyle with the degu.

With proper care and accommodations, your degu may live for eight to twelve years!

It also has to be wary of their mutual predator, the owl. (Because degus are out and about during the day, they have to also be on the lookout for a daytime predator, the hawk.) Chinchilla rats and degus live together in harmony, often seeming oblivious to each other's presence. Degus have been observed to walk right over the top of sleeping chinchilla rats as they go about their daily activities. The chinchilla rat begins its night life about the time the degus are settling in to bed. In the chambers, chinchilla rat babies and degu babies have been found mixed together with either degu or chinchilla rat parents overseeing their activities!

Fortunately, you do not have to duplicate the western slopes of the Andes Mountains or add chinchilla rats to your menagerie to keep your degu happy. Depending upon your lifestyle and the amount of time and space you have available, you can design a housing setup that is convenient for you and as complex or simple as you please. Your pet will be perfectly happy in most of the wide variety of cage styles and glass aquaria available from your local pet store.

You can construct a cage for your degus with materials from the local hardware store. Just be sure there is no way for your pet to chew or squeeze through. Degus enjoy multitiered cages so they can climb and jump. Be sure all lids and doors are securely fastened to prevent escape.

TIP

Minimum Cage Size for One Degu

12 inches wide × 24 inches long × 9 inches high
(31 cm wide × 61 cm long × 23 cm high)

Housing Considerations

There are five important things to keep in mind when deciding how to house your degu.

✔ Degus are very social animals and it is highly recommended that you house at least two degus together.

In the wild, degus live in communities and extended family groups. Social interactions with members of the same species are necessary for the degu to adapt well in captivity and remain healthy. It is also believed that degus form pair bonds. If your pet is housed alone it will become depressed, bored, and possibly aggressive. A lonely, isolated degu may injure or mutilate itself by chewing the hair off of its feet and tail or wound itself by biting its skin. Ideally, you should plan from the beginning to provide housing with sufficient space for at least two animals.

✔ Degus can chew their way out of almost anything. Chewing is an important degu activity. The front teeth (incisors) grow continually throughout life and must be worn down by chewing. For this reason, wood and plastic caging are not suitable for degus.

✔ Degus are strong diggers. In their natural habitat, wild degus build complex tunnels and burrows. Your pet's housing must be made of material strong enough to prevent tunneling and escape.

✔ Degus are excellent climbers and jumpers. Be sure your degu's cage has a secure door and lid.

✔ Degus have the ability to concentrate urine to retain moisture and certain minerals. Your pet's home should be easy to clean, nonporous, and resistant to moisture, salts, and cleansers.

Housing Options

The cage, style, and size you select will depend upon the number of animals you are housing and the amount of space available in your home. Ideally, a multilevel wire cage should be provided because it offers more opportunity to exercise climbing up and down walls and ramps. Another excellent cage option is a two-tiered wire cage on top of an aquarium, with a wire ramp leading from the aquarium floor up to the wire cage. This provides additional play and exploration space for your pets and allows them to select a warmer, sheltered, draft-free environment, when desired. A large wire mesh cage (with an optional removal floor pan), such as a chinchilla cage, also makes a very good home and is easy to clean. Some people like to use a Plexiglas aquarium to house their degus. If this is an option that appeals to you, be sure your degus have enough play space. More than two degus in a 20-gallon (76 L) aquarium can be somewhat crowded, especially when the tank is furnished with an exercise wheel, nest box, toys, and dishes. A tight-fitting, snap-on or clip-on lid is an important feature of aquarium housing because a degu can easily leap right out the top.

Exercise

Degus are very active animals that love to run. In addition to a spacious cage, an exercise wheel should be considered a necessity. Degus need a running wheel for exercise, to maintain body condition, and for social enrichment. It is a great form of entertainment that your degus will use every day, without fail.

Exercise Wheels

There are several sizes and models of exercise wheels. An exercise wheel with a solid floor is sometimes difficult to find in a size large enough to accommodate an adult degu. However, if you have a choice, this style of exercise wheel is preferable to one with wire rungs because it is safer. The degu's tail cannot be pinched in one of the wheel supports. Also, a solid floor is more comfortable for tiny feet. This is especially important for an animal that runs as much as two to three miles a day in a wheel, as many degus do!

Wheels can be free-standing or attach to the cage wall. Before you buy an exercise wheel, decide which model will be most suitable for your degu's home. For example, a free-standing wire wheel can crowd a cage, taking up valuable floor space that could be better used as a play area. More important, free-standing wheels can

Degus appreciate places to explore and branches to climb.

In the wild, degus cover the entrance to their burrows with sticks and rocks. In captivity, grass hay works just as well!

be a potential danger if one degu is running in it and another degu tries to jump on while the wheel is in motion. It is possible for the second animal to become trapped between the support that runs the diameter of the wheel and the vertical bar of the wheel stand. By suspending the wheel by its base from the top of the cage, this hazard is eliminated. Wheels that attach to the side of the cage and have a solid floor and wall are safest, but many of these are made of plastic and your degu can chew and destroy them.

An exercise wheel is such a popular degu toy you might want to consider purchasing two wheels if you are housing several degus together and there is enough space in the cage.

There are other items you can make or purchase to enhance your pet's enjoyment and encourage exercise. These include platforms, tubes, ladders, ramps, and branches to climb.

Degus need safe, nontoxic chew toys to keep their teeth from growing too long.

Degus enjoy taking dust baths together.

Dust Baths

Dust baths are important activities in degu society. In the wild, degus urinate in their dusting areas and then roll in the dust and urine as a way to scent-mark. Degus that are members of the same colony all share the same dusting spot. In this way, they all have the same scent and can identify members of their group by their odor. A dust bath also serves to remove excess oil from the fur and keep the coat and skin healthy.

A fine, clean dust, specifically sold for rodent use (such as chinchilla dust bath) can be purchased from your local pet store. You do not need to buy a specific type of dusting bin for your pet because degus will take a dust bath in almost any kind of container. A mason jar is ideal for dust baths. Just put a few tablespoons of dust in the jar and lay the jar on its side inside the cage. Your degu will waste no time entering the jar and rolling in the dust and the glass walls will prevent most of the dust from wafting throughout the house. If you do not have a mason jar, a small box or a soup bowl will work nicely. Your degu will take its dust bath almost immediately and will roll around and around and jump in and out of the pan

You don't have to worry about grooming your pet. Degus keep themselves very clean!

several times. It will stir up quite a bit of dust when its uses the dust bath, so be sure you have placed the cage in an area where dust will not bother you or anything in the house (computers, electronics). Your degu should be offered a dust bath at least once a week. If you do not remove the dust bath after use, your degu will urinate in it and use it for a litter box until it becomes so damp it will need to be replaced.

Grooming Supplies

You will notice that your degu is meticulously clean so you do not have to worry about bathing or grooming your pet. There is no need to purchase any combs, brushes, or shampoos for it. In fact, a water bath could cause a degu to become chilled and sick. Shampoo products could also make your degu ill. Never use any shampoos or products containing pesticides to kill parasites on the skin. These products are manufactured with larger animals, such as dogs or cats, in mind. The dose of active chemicals in these products could kill your degu. Even shampoos that do not contain pesticides can be harmful. Besides, shampoos and perfumed grooming products will interfere with the degu's natural odors, which play an important role in the degu's social life with regard to behavior, breeding, territoriality, and community activities in the colony.

If you think your degu has a skin condition that needs attention or that it may have parasites in its fur, contact your veterinarian. It is important to know exactly what the problem is. Your veterinarian can tell you if the problem is contagious to your other degus, your other pets, or to you. If treatment is required, your veterinarian will know which product to use and how much is safe to use on such a small animal. This is very important, because even though degus have a greater ability to metabolize certain drugs than do other rodents, many products are toxic to them.

Lighting

Degus are active during the day with peaks of activity in the morning and late afternoon. This activity schedule can change depending on outside influences, such as unlimited availability of an exercise wheel (see Crepuscular Activities, page 21).

So that your pet can fully enjoy the daytime hours, its cage should be placed in an area of your home that is well lit during the day and dark at night. An ideal lighting system would be twelve hours of light during the day and twelve hours of dark at night, but you do not have to follow such a strict schedule if this is not convenient for you.

If you are planning on raising degus, keep in mind that the amount of artificial lighting your female degu receives may affect whether she breeds on her postpartum estrus and how many litters she produces each year (see Raising Degus).

Degus have been known to change their activity schedules to correspond to that of their owners. If you do not work conventional hours, your degu will adapt and still be awake to provide hours of entertainment for you when you return home.

Bottles and Dishes

Water

Fresh water should be available at all times. You can give your degu water in a dish or in a water bottle with a sipper tube.

A water bottle has several advantages over a weighted (heavy-bottom) water dish. A water bottle is less likely to spill or dampen the cage bedding. It can be fastened to the outside of the cage, leaving more cage space available for a play area. A water bottle holds more water than a water dish, reducing the risk that your pet will run out of water during the day or in the event you are absent from home longer than anticipated. And, if your degu has not used a water bottle before, its keen sense of smell will direct it to the water source. It will learn to use the bottle's sipper tube immediately.

Water bottles also have disadvantages that are important to consider in relation to your degu's health. Water bottles are more difficult to clean than water dishes. Sipper tubes can become plugged, making it impossible for your degu to obtain water. Bacteria can grow and multiply in dirty sipper tubes and contaminate the water, causing serious illness and even death in your pet (see Feeding Your Degu).

Food

In the wild, degus eat wherever they find food—on the ground where they forage or in shrubs and bushes they have climbed. If your degu lives in a cage with a solid floor, you can place its food directly on the bottom of the cage. However, a broad-based or weighted dish, made of chew-proof material that is safe for rodents, is recommended so that the food remains clean and there is less waste. Using a dish also makes it easier for you to monitor your pet's food intake and food preferences.

Water bottles and food dishes should be cleaned and refilled daily. Sipper tubes should be checked daily to be sure they are working properly and cleaned thoroughly each day with a round brush.

Toys for Your Degu

Degus are very playful animals. They are active year round and do not hibernate. When housed together they spend much of their recreation time simply interacting with each other. Because of their active and curious nature, you will not only want to keep your degus in a cage large enough for them to play and socialize, but you will also want to give them plenty of safe and interesting toys. Toys are a worthwhile investment in your pets' overall well being, providing additional stimulus for exploration and play. You will enjoy observing firsthand their intelligence and interesting play behavior.

There are a wide variety of rodent toys available from your local pet store, including chew

Degus require hard branches and chew toys to keep their teeth worn correctly.

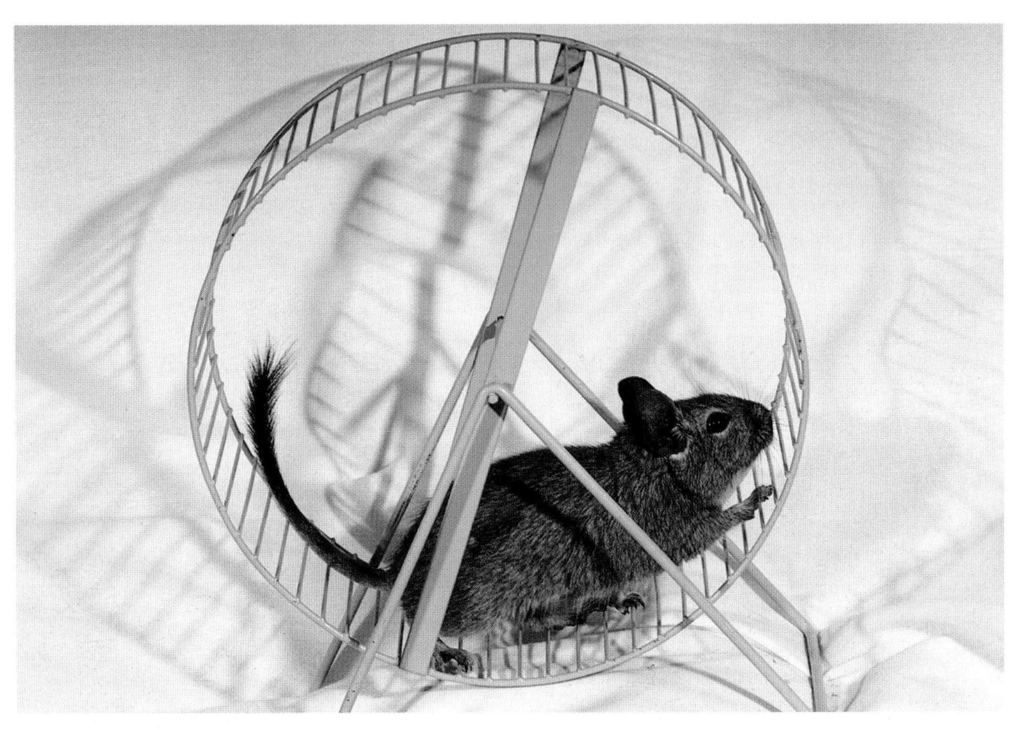

sticks, nest boxes, hideaway houses, ladders, ramps, and tunnel tubes.

Chew Toys

Degus love to chew and because their front teeth grow continually and must be worn down, they need a constant supply of safe rodent chew toys. Degus especially enjoy wooden sticks. It is inherent degu behavior to carry sticks around and stack them at the entries to their homes as an indication of territoriality and ownership. It is best to purchase safe rodent chew sticks from a pet store but if you decide to provide your degus with twigs and sticks, be certain that these materials do not come from any poisonous or potentially harmful plant or tree. Aspen wood makes excellent rodent chew sticks.

Make sure your degu's wheel is designed so that its tail cannot get caught in it and that it is spacious enough that your pet can stretch out when it runs.

Playhouses

Any type of playhouse, nest box, or hideaway house will receive much attention from your pet. Once again, remember that whatever toys you select, your degu will chew on them, so be sure they are made of nontoxic materials.

You may buy tunnel tubes from your local pet store or you can make them yourself from PVC pipe material. PVC is safe for your pet, inexpensive, and can be easily cleaned and reused. Do not use cardboard tubing from paper towel rolls, toilet paper rolls, or gift-wrapping paper rolls. Most of these tubes (98–99 percent) are made from recycled materials and may contain ink residues or other contaminants. Also, it is possible that some of the glues used to make the cardboard tubes may contain toxins.

Degus are very easy to please and will find a creative way to entertain you with almost any safe toy you offer.

Make sure the sipper tube is well within your degu's reach!

Household Hazards

Some of the more fun aspects of degus—their intelligence, small size, activity level, and speed—also create some of the biggest problems for their safety. Because they are small, they are able to fit through spaces you would never think possible. If they can squeeze their head through any crack, the rest of the body follows easily. And because they are so quick, they are excellent escape artists. For these reasons it is impossible to keep a degu in a wooden or cardboard container, even temporarily, because it will chew its way out in no time. Even holding a degu can be a challenge, as it can bounce out of your palms if it is startled. Once your degu is

A nest box or playhouse is a necessity for privacy. Add a ladder to climb and the home is complete!

loose, it faces countless life-threatening situations in your cozy home.

Capturing a runaway degu can be extremely difficult and take a while. Just in case your degu escapes, you need to know what potential household hazards it may encounter so you can correct the situation in advance.

Sticky Traps, Snap Traps, and Rodent Poisons

Go through your house and look for any spaces or holes that your degu can crawl into, as well as anything it can fall into where it can be trapped. And speaking of traps, if you have any sticky or snap traps set in your house or garage, pick them up immediately. Be sure to pick up any rodent bait or poison that may have been left out for wild vermin. They are as deadly for your pet as they are for wild rodents.

Household Chemicals

Degus can hide in cabinets where there are often household products such as cleaning agents, bug sprays, paints, fertilizers, pesticide baits, and other poisonous chemicals. All of these substances are extremely dangerous and potentially deadly for your pet if it comes in contact with them. Some types of paints can be toxic to your pet if it chews on wooden baseboards or walls.

An escaped degu can be hide in almost any small, dark place.

Electrical Shock

Unplug and remove any electrical cords that may be within your escaped degu's reach. Electrocution from gnawing on an electrical cord is a real potential danger that would cost your pet its life and possibly cause an electrical fire.

Appliances

Before you do the laundry, check your clothing, especially the pockets. A laundry basket makes a warm hiding place. Sadly, more than one pocket pet has been found, too late, inside the washer or dryer.

Be very careful when you vacuum under and behind furniture. If you have a powerful built-in vacuum system in your home, and if the vacuum extension has been removed, your pet could easily be sucked down the vacuum hose. As surprising as it sounds, it is not an unusual pocket pet accident!

Other Pets

If you have other pets in the house, remember they pose a serious threat to your degu. A gentle dog or curious cat quickly regains its instincts to hunt or kill small prey, especially when stimulated by the sight of a small animal trying to flee. A fatal accident can take place in a split second. There will also be less chance of your degu coming out of its hiding place if it hears and smells other animals in the area.

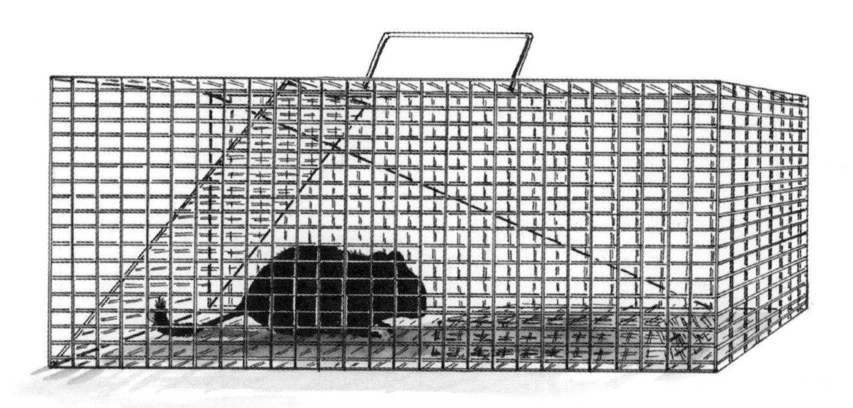

It may be necessary to buy or rent a humane trap in order to catch your escaped pet.

Until your degu is recovered, put your other pets in a secure place where they cannot hurt your degu when it does finally come out of hiding.

If there are small children in the house, ask their assistance in finding the degu. Children are very eager to be helpful and are remarkably skilled at finding the smallest of things. But remind the child not to touch the animal when it is found. A startled degu can inflict a serious bite wound. Also, a small child may inadvertently frighten your pet away before you arrive and capture it.

Outside Doors

Make sure all doors to the outside or the garage are closed. If your degu escapes to the garage, it will be exposed to additional hazards and poisons. For example, your degu might find a few drops of antifreeze (ethylene glycol) on the garage floor. Antifreeze has a sweet taste that appeals to animals, but is a deadly poison that causes kidney failure in a very short time. If your degu escapes to the outdoors, it will be virtually impossible to find it and it will certainly not survive the dangers of automobiles, neighborhood animals, wild birds, and harsh weather conditions.

Crushing Injuries

Everyone in the house must pay close attention to where they step. Your degu can dart out from under an object and be underfoot before you know it. Degus also like to hide in dark places, so inspect your closets and the insides of shoes and boxes. Check the furniture before you sit down on it. Degus can be hiding under the cushions of a couch or chair.

Toilets

Be sure to keep the seat and lid down on the toilet. The same jumping skills that enable your degu to leap out of its cage make it possible for your small pet to leap into the toilet. Once inside the toilet bowl, your degu cannot escape and will become chilled and eventually drown.

Capturing Your Degu

If your degu escapes, but is very tame, you might be able to capture it by setting its cage or

Always keep a fine-mesh net on hand, in case your degu escapes.

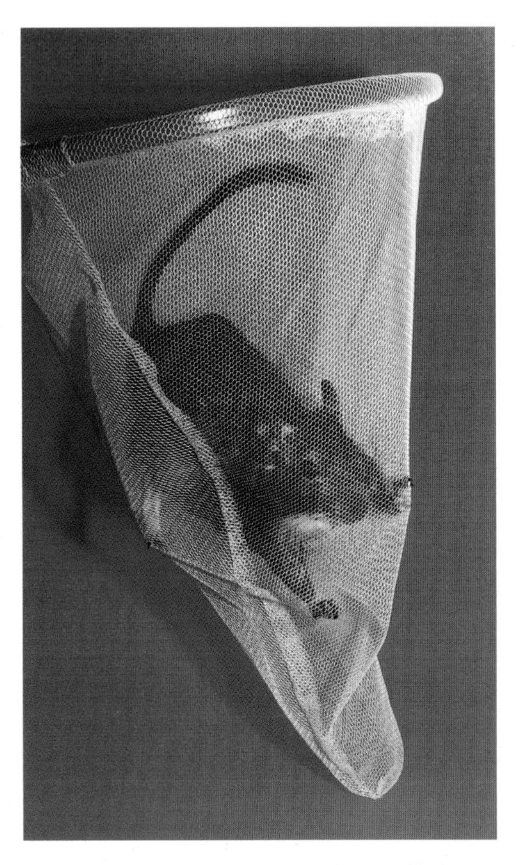

nest box on the floor. Leave an opening to the cage or nest box and bait it with your pet's favorite treat, then leave the area. It helps to turn down the lights and be very quiet. This helps your degu to calm down after the excitement of its escape and free run of the house. If your pet is tired and hungry, and you are very lucky, it may return to its home to eat and rest.

If your degu doesn't come home on its own, you will have to actively look for it before it gets into trouble. Be prepared to capture your degu when you do find it. Have a tightly woven fish or butterfly net with a long handle available to quickly place over it. If you don't have a net it will be very difficult to trap your degu. You can try using a small sheet as a net to throw over your pet. Once the cloth is over the animal, you must act quickly to roll the degu up in the material and transfer it to its cage. You can also try using a box to place over your degu, but this can be cumbersome and you might accidentally injure your pet in the process.

A good option is to purchase a small humane trap, such as a Hav-A-Hart trap, at the local pet shop or feed store. If you cannot purchase a trap, you may be able to rent or borrow one from your local animal shelter or veterinarian. Bait the trap with your degu's favorite treat (raisins, apples, and sunflower seeds are very popular) and place it in an easily accessible and quiet area.

If you are using a trap, you are most likely to catch your degu during the early morning or early evening hours when it is most active. It will probably be hidden and sleeping during the night.

Whatever kind of traps you use, be sure to check them several times a day. By the time you catch your degu it may be very hungry and thirsty and may need immediate care.

Degus love tunnels, and a plastic tunnel allows you to watch the fun!

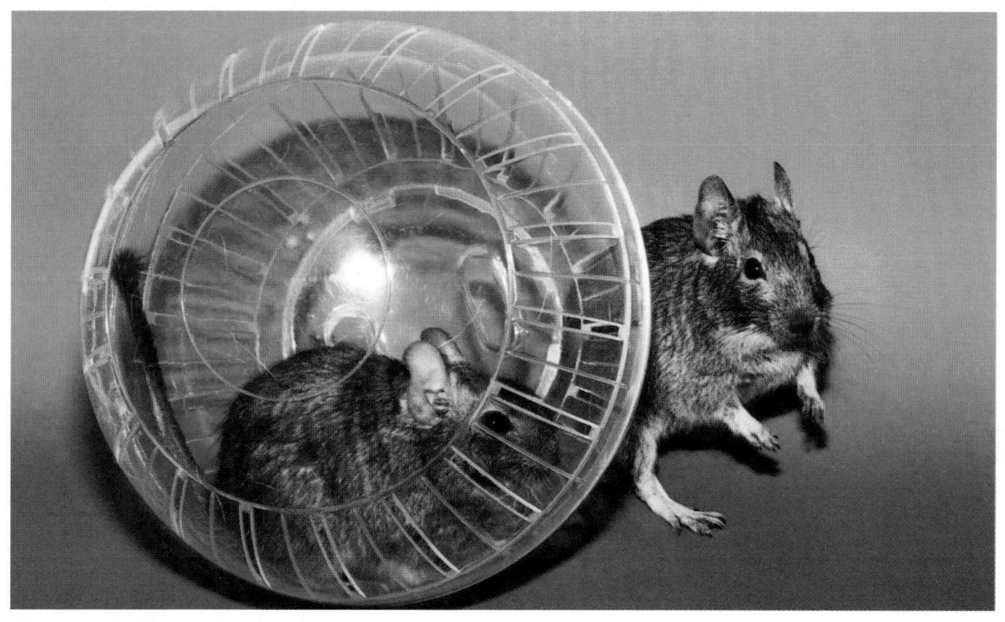

Hamster balls are fun for degus, too!

HOW-TO: CAGE FEATURES

Recommended Cage Features

One of the most important features to consider when you are selecting a cage for your pet is the ease in which you can access and capture it from the cage interior. *Never pick your degu up by its tail.* A spectacular and effective degu defense behavior is that when lifted by its tail, a degu will spin around and around like a top until the tail sheath separates and the tail disconnects from the body. In the wild, by losing its tail, the degu may save its life by being able to escape from a predator. Unfortunately the tail will not grow back. The cage you select must allow you easy access to your pet, with ample space to use both hands to scoop up your degu without damaging its tail. If your cage is tall or multi-tiered and has only one opening, it is more convenient if the door is located on the front of the cage, rather than the top.

Degus are more comfortable living directly on bedding, as opposed to being elevated above the floor pan and housed directly on a wire floor. You can fill the floor pan full of shavings so they make a firm support under the wire floor and spread shavings on top of the wire floor if needed. If cage design prevents you from housing your degus directly on wood shavings, give your pets a footrest area by providing them with a flat piece of pinewood. If your degu does not have a solid surface to rest its feet, it can develop sores (commonly known as "bumblefoot") from the continual pressure of the wire mesh floor against its feet. Be sure that the wood you place in the cage has not been chemically treated or preserved, as is done for wooden boards used in construction. Chemicals and preservatives can be toxic to your pet. The board should also be free of staples, nails, and any other foreign object that can be chewed or swallowed. Of course, you will have to periodically replace the wooden footrest because your degu will eventually chew it up!

If your degu is housed directly on top of a wire floor, make sure the mesh spacing is large enough to allow waste material to drop through to the floor pan, but small enough to prevent your pet's feet from getting caught or injured in between the wire mesh.

Degus are good climbers and jumpers. They can leap surprisingly high and escape from most enclosures so it is important to house them in a well-enclosed cage with a secure, latching door or lid.

Bedding Material

Aspen shavings are recommended for bedding material. If you cannot find aspen shavings, pine shavings usually work well for degu bedding. Although some types of pine shavings may cause itchy skin or other problems, most pine shavings make suitable cage bedding material and are preferable to cedar shavings. Cedar shavings smell nice and look pretty, but they may cause medical conditions such as itchy skin, respiratory problems, and even possible liver problems. For these reasons, it is recommended that you do not use cedar shavings in your pet's cage.

Only shavings that are packaged and indicated for use as bedding material for caged pets should be used in your degu's cage. Shavings that are sold for horse stalls or stored in open outdoor bins may be contaminated with undesirable material or even urine and germs from wild rodents. These shavings can pose a health risk for your pet and possibly contain rodent disease organisms.

Shavings absorb urine and odors and should be changed at least once a week. If several animals are housed together, the shavings may need to be replaced twice a week or more often as necessary.

Be sure that the bedding material you use is as dust-free as possible. Bedding that contains a lot of dust and fine particles can be very irritating to your degu's lungs and cause wheezing, sneezing, and other respiratory problems.

Nesting Material

Degus are not as elaborate nest builders as some rodents, but they do enjoy the activity. They are perfectly happy with a hideaway, some bedding, some small sticks, and a little bit of grass or alfalfa hay. Degus in the wild are territorial. They live in underground burrows with other members of their community and build mounds near the burrow entrances to signify ownership. The mounds are comprised of sticks, small rocks, grass, and dung. In captivity, grass or hay can be used for nesting material, as long as it is fresh, dry, and free of dust and mold.

Nest Box

Every cage should contain a nest box. The nest box is where your degu will spend its private time sleeping, resting, and snuggling with friends and family. A wooden nest box with a hinged lid gives your degu the darkness, warmth, and quiet it would experience in an underground burrow. If your degu has babies or you need to check on your pet for any reason, you can lift the lid just enough to take a peek at them.

Even though the nest box is wooden, degus with plenty of chew toys usually do not chew excessively on their nest box.

Degus can run fast, climb, and jump very high. Be sure your degu's cage top is securely fastened to prevent escape.

Temperature and Humidity

In the wild, degus live in a subtropical to temperate region. In captivity, they are quite comfortable at room temperature (69–72°F, 20°C). Degus should be protected from drafts, extreme temperature variations, and excessive dryness. Humidity should be no less than 40 percent to avoid skin problems and other possible medical problems. For baby degus, humidity should ideally be at least 50–55 percent to avoid dehydration. Exchange of fresh air is also important. Degus require well-ventilated, but not drafty, enclosures. They should not be placed near heaters, radiators, or fans, or in areas of direct sunlight. This is especially critical for degus housed in glass aquaria where exposure to direct sunlight can elevate temperatures beyond the comfort and safety zone (greenhouse effect).

FEEDING YOUR DEGU

The wild degu's diet consists of whatever grasses, leaves, bark, seeds, bulbs, tubers, fruits, and roots it can find within its reach. The degu's taste for prickly pear cactus, wheat grain, cornstalks, fruit, and produce from vineyards and orchards has made it an agricultural pest in parts of Chile where farms overlap degu territory.

Because degus are not fussy eaters and will readily eat a wide variety of plants, seeds, roots, and grains, providing a balanced, nutritious diet for your degu is extremely easy.

What to Feed

Proper nutrition plays an important role in your pet's overall health, life span, and reproduction. The majority of the diet should consist of a balanced, high-quality commercial rodent food, for example, a mixture of rat chow and guinea pig pellets. Be sure the food you provide is fresh and check daily to be certain any food your degu has hidden and stashed is free of mold. Store all food in closed containers in a cool, dry place.

Commercial Rodent Food

Degus are basically vegetarians and thrive on the large selection of rodent chows commercially available from pet stores. Most of your degu's diet should consist of commercial rodent chow provided free choice (also called free feeding, or *ad libidum*), which means around-the-clock food availability. Degus enjoy rodent blocks, a balanced rodent diet manufactured into small, hard blocks. They are nutritious and help wear down the teeth. Some research laboratories prefer to feed degus a combination of rodent chow and guinea pig chow supplemented with carrots, sunflower seeds, apples, and a few peanuts. Guinea pig chow is fed because it is enriched with vitamin C and some people have observed that members of the Hystricomorph family (which includes degus) do well with supplemental vitamin C, although to date it has not been demonstrated that this supplementation is a necessity.

Freshness: Be sure the food you provide is fresh. To ensure the freshness of the rodent diet or guinea pig diet you purchase, check the milling date on the food package to verify the shelf life of the product. If the food is old,

Degus are eager eaters and enjoy a healthy treat now and then.

the vitamins in the food will lose their potency and no longer be effective. This is especially true for vitamin C. Although standard laboratory recommendations are to feed chow that is no older than six months (180 days) from the time of milling, it would be wiser to discard any food that is more than 30 days old. This is because once the food package has been opened and the food has been exposed to atmospheric conditions, vitamin C begins to lose its potency very rapidly. Play it safe. Be sure the guinea pig chow you feed your degu is not older than one month from the time of milling.

Seeds, Grains, Hay, and Treats

Your degu will enjoy various treats of seeds and grains, which should be raw and unsalted. Degus also enjoy grass hay and alfalfa hay, available in small bales or packages at your pet store. What is a degu's favorite treat? It depends on the animal, but it is hard to find something degus love more than raisins, a delicacy wild degus enjoy out in the vineyards of Chile. When you feed your degus fruits and vegetables, be sure to remove the remainders from the cage before they spoil.

Whatever you feed your degu, make sure a quality commercial rodent chow and guinea pig chow make up the majority of the diet and limit treats to a reasonable amount. Avoid feeding too many treats, especially those high in sugar content. If your degu consumes too many treats, it will eat less of its rodent chow and will not receive a balanced diet. It will also be more prone to medical problems such as obesity and diabetes.

A combination of fresh rodent food, hay, seeds, nuts, grains, and raw fruits and vegetables make mealtime interesting and nutritious and will help keep your degu healthy.

Vitamins and Minerals

If your pet is receiving a good balanced commercial rodent diet, and if you are feeding fresh raw fruits (apples and raisins), and vegetables (carrots, collard greens, kale, lettuce, tomatoes), grains (wheat germ), and seeds (sunflower seeds, sesame seeds, pumpkin seeds, peanuts), there should be no need to supplement meals with mineral and vitamin additives. In fact, oversupplementation of vitamins and minerals can cause health problems. If you wish to provide vitamin C for your degu, you can feed it a small amount of fresh orange, peach, apricot, or pear in season. Remember not to feed an excessive amount of fruits, as these are high in sugar content.

A mixture of commercial rodent chow and guinea pig chow makes a nutritionally balanced degu diet.

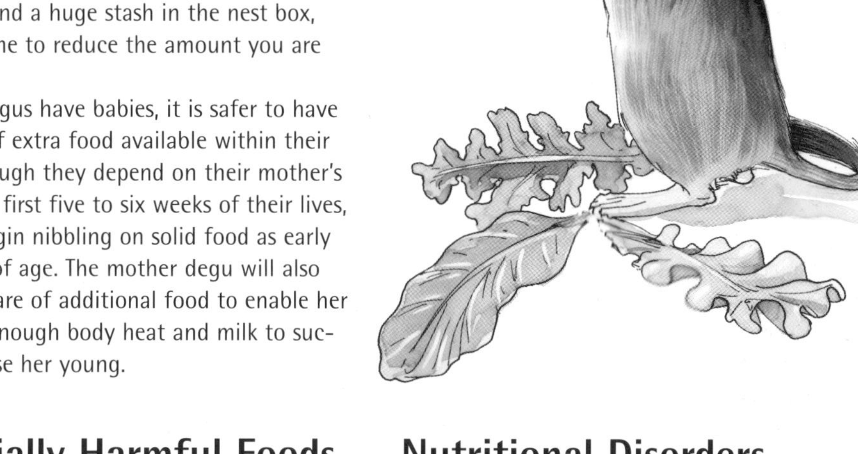
Degus enjoy a wide variety of greens.

How Much and How Often

Degus are eager eaters. They burn up a lot of calories with all their activities and require even more food if they are growing, pregnant, or nursing their young. Degus will stockpile food in their nest box for safekeeping. It is all right for them to hide away a little bit of food, but if you find a huge stash in the nest box, then it is time to reduce the amount you are feeding.

If your degus have babies, it is safer to have a little bit of extra food available within their reach. Although they depend on their mother's milk for the first five to six weeks of their lives, they will begin nibbling on solid food as early as one day of age. The mother degu will also need her share of additional food to enable her to provide enough body heat and milk to successfully raise her young.

Potentially Harmful Foods

Do not feed your degus cooked or processed foods. These are not good for them and may be lacking in vitamins or contain food additives and preservatives. Do not feed your degus chocolate (which contains theobromine, a product similar to caffeine) or other candies. If you are not sure about the safety or nutritional benefit of any food type, simply do not feed it to your pet. If you wish to provide a special "treat" other than fresh vegetables, fruits, or seeds, be sure to purchase commercial products from the pet store that are made especially for rodents.

Nutritional Disorders

Rodent nutritional requirements have been studied extensively and are available from publications of the National Academy of Sciences and various feed companies. However, to date, the nutritional requirements of degus have not been precisely determined. A combination of quality rat chow and guinea pig chow appears to provide a balanced diet.

If your degu does not receive proper nutrition or a nutritionally balanced diet, it can suffer from a variety of health problems, including weak teeth (white or light in color), diabetes, weight loss, or obesity.

Corn is not only a degu delicacy, it helps wear down sharp teeth and keeps them healthy.

If you feed your degu a balanced diet, there will be no need to give it vitamin or mineral supplements.

Left: Feed sweet fruits in moderation. Eating too much sugar can lead to health problems.

Below left: Make sure your degu has fresh water every day.

Below right: To be sure your degu has pure, clean, chemical-free drinking water, you may give it bottled water for human consumption—the same water you buy to make your coffee or tea.

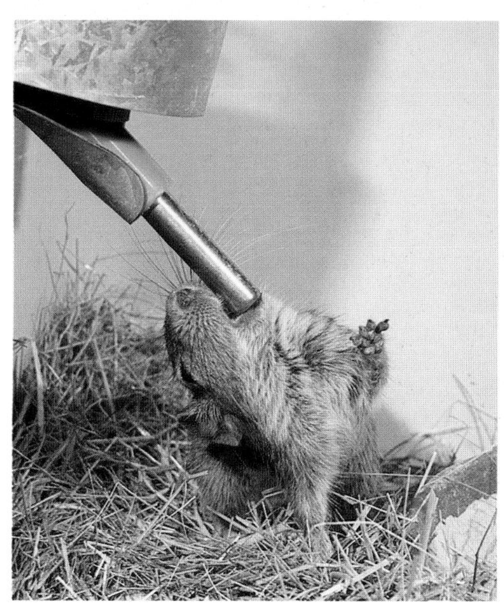

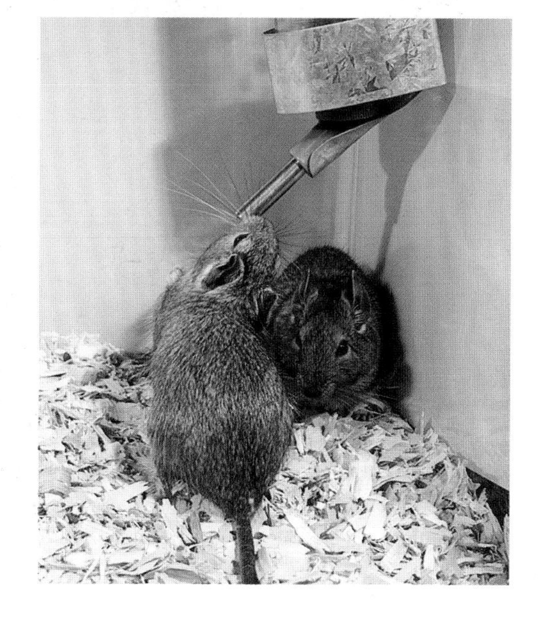

TIP

Water

✔ Give your degu fresh water every day.

✔ As a safety precaution to prevent bacterial growth and reduce water contamination, you should chlorinate your pet's water. Most research laboratories that house degus and other rodents use the following formula to obtain chlorination at 10 to 12 parts per million:

1 ml of 5.25 percent sodium hypochlorite solution (bleach) in 5 liters of water.

Unless you have many degus and several water bottles to fill, you will not need 5 liters (almost 5 quarts) of water, so another way to chlorinate the water is:

Add one drop of bleach to one quart or one liter of water, mix well, fill your degu's water bottle or dish, and discard the rest of the water.

✔ Keep an extra water bottle and sipper tube on hand so you will always have a clean set ready to alternate each day.

Water

Depending upon where you live, contents of city or well water may vary and could contain additives such as chlorine and chloramine, or high levels of undesirable elements, such as arsenic, or low levels of bacteria. The best water you can provide your pet is the same drinking water you filter or buy for yourself. Do not give your pet distilled, demineralized, or deionized water. Just like humans, animals require natural minerals found in spring water. Commercial bottled drinking water is an inexpensive and safe way to ensure the health of your pet.

Be aware of the following:

✔ Degus should have access to pure, clean drinking water at all times. Water is especially important because most of your pet's diet is dry (pellets, seeds, rodent blocks) and a dry diet increases the need for water. Your degu will readily drink from a water dish or a sipper tube.

✔ Water consumption depends on your pet's health, condition, and age. It is also greatly influenced by its activity level and reproductive cycle. If your degu is pregnant or nursing babies, she may drink more than twice the amount of water she usually does. Room temperature and humidity also affect how much water your degu consumes. Animals housed in a warm, dry room will drink more than those in cooler, more humid environments.

✔ Always provide more water than your degu normally drinks. If you are housing

Always check to be sure the sipper tube on the water bottle is not leaking or plugged with bedding material.

several animals together, be sure the water supply is sufficient to provide the animals all the water they will need, plus a little extra.

✔ If your degu is receiving water from a water bottle, check the sipper tube daily to be certain it is functioning properly and is not plugged. Many animal deaths have been due to sipper tubes that were plugged with bedding material or debris, denying water access to a thirsty pet.

✔ Degus can become very ill and die from *Pseudomonas* bacteria found in contaminated water. Keep your pet's water dishes, bottles, and sipper tubes meticulously clean and provide fresh water daily.

Baby Degus

If you have baby degus fourteen days of age or older, they should also have access to a source of moisture. Although they are not weaned from their mother's milk until they are five to six weeks of age, and should not be separated from their mother before four weeks of age, they must learn how to use a sipper tube or water bottle early in life. Your baby degus will start investigating water sources at about two weeks of age. At that time you can provide a small amount of fresh, raw, moist carrot, lettuce, or apple. (Potato is sometimes used as a moisture source for young rodents; however, your baby degus would prefer something less starchy and tastier, such as sweet potato, yam, or jicama. If you do give your degus raw potato, be sure any green parts and the "potato eyes" are removed, as these contain a poison called solanine). At the end of the day, remember to check your pet's food storage areas and discard old vegetable or fruit so it does not rot or soil the cage.

You should also lower the water bottle so that the sipper tube is 1 to 2 inches (2.5–5 cm) above the cage floor, within reach of the baby degus. Make sure the sipper tube is not so low that it comes in contact with the cage bedding. If this happens, the sipper tube can either become plugged or the water may completely wick out into the bedding material. Even worse, a plugged sipper tube is an invitation for bacterial growth and water contamination.

Cleaning

To prevent water contamination, the water dish or bottle should be thoroughly cleaned, rinsed well, and refilled daily. If you are using a water bottle, pay particular attention to the cleanliness of the sipper tube. Bacteria rapidly multiply in sipper tubes, especially when they are plugged with small particles and contaminants. Clean your degu's dishes and bottles with a mild detergent, like the one you use for your own dishes. Rinse them thoroughly to completely remove all traces of the detergent. You can also soak the bottle and sipper tube for a few minutes in mildly chlorinated water, then rinse them thoroughly several times. If you prefer, you can use boiling water to rinse the water bottle and soak the sipper tube. When the water bottle and sipper tube are rinsed well, and completely cooled, fill the water bottle with commercial bottled drinking water sold for human consumption.

HEALTH

The most important health care you can provide your degu is preventive. Preventing problems is much easier than treating problems.

Keeping Your Degu Healthy

Degus are very hardy animals. With good care your degu should stay healthy into its old age. But if it becomes ill, it will need immediate attention. Without care, a sick degu can quickly weaken and die.

Signs of a Sick Degu

Sometimes even the best-cared-for animals become ill. Successful recovery depends upon the type of illness and how early the illness was noticed and treated. To recognize a sick degu, you must first know how a healthy degu looks and acts. If your pet is acting sluggish, has a dull coat, is hunched up in an abnormal posture, or is not eating or drinking, then there is most certainly a problem. The sooner you have the problem diagnosed and begin treatment, the better your pet's chances of recovery.

The table on page 67 lists some ways to tell if your degu is healthy or not.

A healthy degu is alert, bright-eyed, and interested in its surroundings.

If Your Degu Is Sick

1. The first thing you should do, the moment you notice your pet is ill, is separate it from any other pets you have. This way, if the problem is contagious, you have reduced the chances of spreading disease to your other animals.

2. Isolating your sick degu gives it a chance to begin its recuperation in peace and quiet without distraction and stress.

3. Place your degu in a comfortable, dark, quiet place.

4. Continue to keep a close watch on your other degus and separate out any others that may also become ill.

5. Wash thoroughly all housing, toys, dishes, and bottles that were in contact with your sick pet. Discard old food and used bedding and nesting material.

6. Wash your hands thoroughly after handling any sick animal and before handling other pets or food. This will help prevent the possible spread of contagious disease.

7. Contact your veterinarian for advice. An examination is important to diagnose the problem. It is the only way to know exactly

A sick degu looks ruffled and acts dull. The bright, alert look is gone. It does not want to eat, play, or be handled.

what the problem is and if it is contagious to you or your other pets. A prescription medication may be indicated to ensure your pet's survival. Degus are resistant to some medications and sensitive to others, so your veterinarian's expertise is necessary. Since handling and transportation can further upset your sick pet, your veterinarian may make a house call. If you must transport your degu, it is less stressful if the degu can travel in its nest box, if possible. Cover the box with a large towel to reduce sounds and light that might startle your small companion.

TIP

Essentials of Good Degu Care

- ✔ Good, nutritious food and fresh water
- ✔ Plenty of space to run and play
- ✔ Clean, dry, draft-free housing
- ✔ Comfortable temperature and humidity
- ✔ Nest box
- ✔ Chew toys to keep teeth healthy
- ✔ Exercise wheel
- ✔ Interesting toys
- ✔ Another degu to keep it company
- ✔ Lots of attention from you

Helping Your Veterinarian Help You

Make a list of all the questions you want to ask your veterinarian. Your veterinarian will also ask you some questions to help make a diagnosis and determine an appropriate treatment. Don't worry if you don't have all the answers; every piece of information will be helpful for your pet.

Before your appointment, make a list of the following information:

- ✔ How old is your degu?
- ✔ How long have you owned your pet?
- ✔ When did you first notice the problem?
- ✔ Does your pet appear to be in any discomfort or pain?
- ✔ What, if anything, have you given or done to treat the problem?
- ✔ When did your degu last eat or drink?
- ✔ Has there been a change in your pet's diet or living environment?
- ✔ When did your degu last have a bowel movement?
- ✔ Does your degu have a normal stool, constipation, or diarrhea?
- ✔ Is there any staining or caked feces around the anus or perineum?
- ✔ Are there any other animals at home? If so, what kind and how many?

Ways to Tell If Your Degu Is Healthy

	Healthy Degu	*Sick Degu*
Appearance	Bright, clear eyes	Dull expression, eyes partially closed
	Well-groomed, shiny coat	Ruffled coat in poor condition
	Yellow-orange teeth	Pale yellow or white teeth
	Robust, compact	Thin, losing weight
Behavior	Alert, active, very sociable	Lethargic, depressed, slow
	Good appetite	Will not eat or drink
	Sits, stands, climbs, jumps, runs in exercise wheel, explores, and plays	Hunched-up position, inactive
		Quiet
	Vocalizes frequently	

✔ How many animals are housed in the same cage with your sick degu?
✔ If you have any other pets, did you purchase any of them recently?
✔ Do any of your other pets have any problems that seem similar or related?
✔ What do you feed your degu (including special treats)?
✔ How is your degu housed?
✔ What is the cage-cleaning schedule?
✔ Has your pet been exposed to any sick animals or chemicals?
✔ Where did you obtain your pet?
✔ If your degu is a female, is it pregnant or when did it last produce a litter?
✔ Add any other findings or relevant information.

Health Problems

Degus can contract a variety of bacterial, viral, and fungal infections. They may be troubled by external (skin, hair, ears) and internal (intestinal) parasites. Degus may also suffer from noncontagious medical conditions, such as cataracts, diabetes, cancer, and genetic disorders.

Bite Wounds

Degus are mild-mannered and nonaggressive. Although during a confrontation they may chatter their teeth, growl, and squeak, they rarely actually bite one another. You can reduce the incidence of bite wounds by making sure your animals are not overcrowded and that the animals you do house together are compatible. Do not house two males together unless they have been raised together since birth.

Because degus have such long, sharp teeth, bite wounds can be a serious injury. Deep puncture wounds frequently become infected and form abscesses.

To check your degu for bite wounds, push the fur back with your fingers and look for any lumps, bumps, puncture holes, swelling, redness, tenderness, or pus. If a bite wound is deep, it can cause muscle and nerve damage.

Treatment: Clean the wound with a mild antiseptic solution or hydrogen peroxide. Keep the wound clean and allow it to drain until it has closed on its own and healed.

Dehydration

Dehydration occurs when an animal loses too much water from the body. There are many causes of dehydration, including not drinking enough water, illness and diarrhea, and exposure to a hot, dry environment.

Treatment: The treatment for dehydration is rehydration, which is replenishing the body with water. When an animal becomes dehydrated, it also loses minerals from its body. If your pet is dehydrated, give it immediate access to fresh drinking water. Do not try to force water on your pet if it is unconscious or too weak to drink on its own, because it may aspirate the water into its lungs. Contact your veterinarian immediately and ask if a balanced electrolyte solution, a mixture of water and necessary minerals in the proper dilution for rehydration, is advised. Electrolyte solutions are available from your veterinarian. In an emergency, you can also find electrolyte solutions formulated for human babies, available at pharmacies and supermarkets. Keep a bottle on hand in case of emergency.

Note: Do not give your pet homemade salt or sugar mixtures without consulting your veterinarian. In the wrong proportions, these will do more harm than good by further dehydrating your pet.

Dental Problems

The outer surface of the incisors is harder than the inside material, so as your degu chews,

If your degu becomes dehydrated, offer it fresh water immediately.

Social interactions play an important role in your degu's health and well-being.

Degus are active and athletic. Climbing is good exercise for a healthy degu.

its teeth are constantly chiseled and sharpened. There are no nerves in the incisors, except at the base of the tooth where growth takes place.

If your degu is very tame, and if you feel comfortable handling your pet, you can check its mouth regularly for dental problems. You can do this by holding it with one hand and gently lifting its upper lips with your other hand, revealing the front incisors. Never place yourself in danger of being accidentally bitten. If you prefer, your veterinarian can perform the dental examination for you.

Most dental problems can be avoided by providing safe chew toys, a balanced diet sufficient in calcium, and by removing animals with dental problems from the breeding program.

White teeth: As surprising as it sounds, if a degu has white teeth, it is an indication of poor health. Degu teeth should be dark yellow to orange in color. White teeth may be caused by illness or nutritional inadequacies.

Malocclusion: When the incisors do not grow in proper alignment, the teeth wear unevenly. This is called "malocclusion" and may be an inherited problem. One or more of the misdirected incisors may grow into the tissues of the mouth. This painful condition can make it difficult or impossible for the degu to eat. Signs of malocclusion may include protruding teeth, lack of appetite, weight loss, and a swollen, painful mouth.

Treatment. The offending tooth may be trimmed back. Although you can do this yourself using small animal nail clippers, you run the risk of accidentally fracturing the incisor. Your veterinarian can safely trim the tooth back using appropriate dental tools. No anesthetic is required because there is no sensation in the upper part of the tooth. The dental tool is placed over the tooth and aligned where the cut is intended. If you elect to do the procedure yourself, check to be sure the tongue, lips,

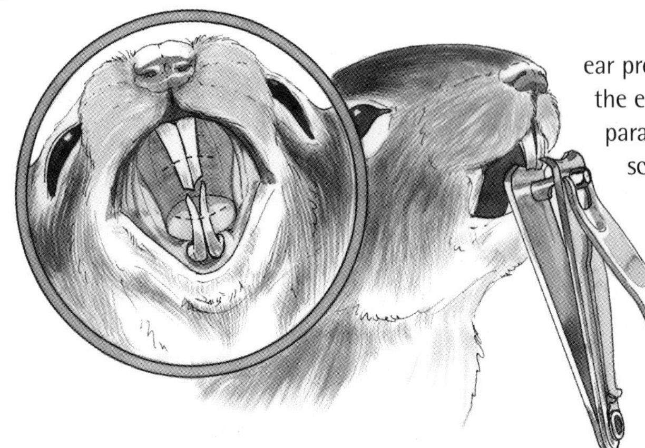

If your degu's teeth are overgrown, your veterinarian can show you how to trim them with a pair of nail cutters. Don't worry! It doesn't hurt!

and cheeks are out of the way. If you feel uncomfortable doing this, ask your veterinarian to do it or to show you how.

The tooth will grow back and will need to be trimmed regularly. Degus that have dental malocclusion should not be used for breeding because this condition may be inherited.

Broken teeth: Sometimes an incisor may break. It will grow back, but during that time, the tooth opposite the missing or broken tooth may become overgrown because it has nothing to grind against. You may need to trim the opposite tooth until the broken tooth grows back.

Gum infection and tooth loss: Once in a while the gums may become infected and a tooth may require removal. Your degu may have a swollen mouth and refuse to eat. Dental extraction is a job for your veterinarian!

Ear Problems

Even though your pet's ears are relatively large, it is not always easy to tell if it is having ear problems because it is difficult to see inside the ear canal. Ear problems may be caused by parasites, infection, or injury. Signs include scratching at the ears, head shaking, tilting the head to one side, and loss of balance.

Treatment: Place a drop of mineral oil on a cotton-tipped swab and gently wipe away any dirt or debris from your degu's ears. This may also give your pet some relief from itching. If the problem is due to infection or parasites or if it persists, you will probably need a professional evaluation, cleansing, and treatment with a prescription medication from your veterinarian to treat the disease. If your pet's condition appears to be painful, contact your veterinarian immediately. Signs of pain include loss of appetite, nervousness, irritability, inactivity, continued scratching or licking at the affected area, head tilting, or squeaking (vocalizing) when handled.

Eye Problems

Eye problems may develop from injury, infection, or irritating substances. Check your pet daily to be sure its eyes are clear and bright. If your degu's eyes are dull, have a discharge, or are closed, place your degu in a dark room and contact your veterinarian. Many eye problems are painful or make the eyes sensitive to light. Your veterinarian can provide an appropriate, gentle eyewash and eye ointment or drops, if necessary.

Many eye problems look similar. For example, both ulcers of the cornea and cataracts give the eyes a cloudy appearance. Some eye problems cannot be treated or may be signs of additional health problems. For example, cataracts are frequently seen in diabetic animals. For this reason, you should avoid feeding your pet sugary treats and keep your degu's sugar consumption to a minimum to prevent or slow the development of diabetes and cataracts.

Treatment: Many eye conditions are very painful and most require veterinary expertise, so make an appointment with your veterinarian immediately. Light may hurt your degu's eyes so place it in a dark room until your veterinary appointment. Unfortunately, there is no treatment or cure for cataracts in pet degus.

Gastrointestinal Problems

Stomach and intestinal problems can be caused by bacterial or viral infections, parasites, improper diet, stress, or unsanitary housing conditions. These problems are often painful conditions and can cause bloat, constipation, or diarrhea.

Bloat: Bloat is the accumulation of gas within the gastrointestinal tract. Gas and fluid accumulate, causing the abdomen to swell and distend. There are a variety of causes of bloat, including bacterial, viral, and protozoan infections, as well as obstructions of the gastrointestinal tract. Bloat should always be considered an emergency situation. It is extremely painful and can result in death in a short period of time.

Treatment. Contact your veterinarian immediately. This is an emergency situation and treatment will vary according to the severity and cause.

Constipation: Constipation is difficulty passing dry, hard feces. Causes of constipation include dehydration, insufficient water intake, dry or hot environment, obstruction of the intestinal tract, and parasitism.

Treatment. Be sure your degu can reach the water bottle and that the sipper tube is functioning properly. Remove all dry food and replace it with moist food, such as apple or lettuce, until the stools return to normal. Consult your veterinarian.

Diarrhea: Disease, infection, stress, or an excess of fruits and vegetables in the diet can all cause diarrhea. If not treated quickly, diarrhea can in turn cause rapid dehydration and even death. The feces are soft, mucus, or liquid and the anal area may be wet and soiled.

Treatment. If your degu has diarrhea, it may need medicine to recover. Stop feeding any fruits or vegetables and ask your veterinarian for a balanced electrolyte solution for rehydration. Consult your veterinarian.

Heatstroke

Degus can become overheated and suffer from heatstroke. Be sure that your degu's cage is not in direct sunlight and is not close to any fireplaces or heaters. If you must transport your pet, never leave it in the car. On a warm day, a car can heat up to 120°F (48.9°C) in a few minutes, even with the windows partially open. Adequate ventilation is also important to prevent your pet from becoming too hot.

If your degu is exposed to high temperatures, it will quickly become weak, unresponsive, and eventually comatose. Without immediate emergency treatment it will die. You will have to quickly and safely drop your degu's temperature. Then you will have to rehydrate your pet.

Treatment: To cool down your degu, hold it in your hand in a sink of cool (not cold) water. Be sure to keep its head above water so it can safely breathe. Once your degu has regained consciousness, dry it gently and place it in a dry, dark, comfortable cage to rest. Next, rehydrate your degu with a balanced electrolyte solution.

Make sure your degu is fully conscious and able to swallow so that the solution does not go into its lungs. Consult your veterinarian after you have cooled your degu.

Injury and Trauma

Small animals have a way of sometimes being in the wrong place at the wrong time. If your degu is dropped, stepped on, attacked by the family dog or cat, or injured in any way, try to determine how seriously it is hurt. Isolate it in a clean, comfortable cage. Do not handle your degu more than necessary. Observe it closely to be sure it acts and moves about normally and continues to eat and drink. Contact your veterinarian for advice.

Nails

Busy degus keep their nails worn down. They also chew their nails to keep them neat and trim. However, a nail can become caught or snagged in something, tear, and bleed. Unless the nail bed has been damaged, it will grow back. In the meantime, the injury should be kept clean to prevent infection.

Cataracts give the eyes a cloudy appearance and can be a sign of additional health problems, such as diabetes.

Treatment: A torn nail may be trimmed carefully using nail clippers designed for human babies. These small clippers work well for tiny degu nails. When you trim your pet's torn nail, just trim the very tip of it to prevent bleeding and additional damage.

Respiratory Problems

If you hear your degu wheezing or sneezing, take these symptoms seriously. Contact your veterinarian immediately. Your pet may have developed an allergy or fine, powdery bedding may be irritating its respiratory tract. In more serious cases, your degu may have been exposed to dangerous germs or to a damp, cold, drafty environment. Whatever the initial cause, your degu could develop pneumonia. Signs of pneumonia include breathing difficulty, discharge from the eyes and nose, lack of appetite, inactivity, and weight loss. Pneumonia is a serious disease that can cause death if it is not treated immediately with the proper medication. Consult your veterinarian.

Skin and Fur Problems

Signs of skin problems include: loss of fur; sores; dry, flaky, itchy skin; and moist, oozing, reddened skin. Skin problems may be caused by tiny skin parasites, allergies, hormonal imbalance, improper diet, disease, or fungal and bacterial infections. Your veterinarian's expertise is necessary to diagnose the exact cause of your pet's condition. Often a specific prescription medication is required to treat the problem successfully.

The degu's toes are covered with long, stiff, white hairs. Trim only the tips of the nails.

Your degu's large eyes and ears make them easy to examine for signs of a problem.

Unavoidable Problems

Some medical conditions, such as problems with the heart, kidneys, liver, or other internal organs, may go unnoticed. Many problems associated with aging or genetics, such as diabetes or cancer, cannot be prevented. If your pet has a medical problem you cannot treat or cure, you can still provide the best home remedy of all—good food and a safe, comfortable, loving home.

Normal Conditions Commonly Mistaken for Problems

Degus have some normal conditions that are often mistaken for problems. Don't let them fool you!

Urine: Normal degu urine is yellow and thick and may be mistaken for pus

Vaginal closure membrane: When the female degu is pregnant or isolated from the male, a small membrane covers the entrance to the vagina. This membrane may open and seal closed again periodically throughout gestation. This is normal and not a cause for concern.

On the lookout and curious about what's going on...there is no doubt that this degu is in excellent health!

Degu Health Check Sheet

Health Problem	*Symptoms*	*Causes*
Bite wounds	Sores, redness, swelling, infection, pain or tenderness, draining pus	Fighting among incompatible animals, overcrowding
Bloat	Distended abdomen, filled with gas and fluid, extreme pain, lack of appetite, inactivity	Can be due to protozoan parasite *Giardia*, bacterial or viral infections, improper nutrition, unsanitary housing conditions, stress
Broken teeth	Tooth breaks and tooth opposite overgrows into mouth tissue causing pain and inability to eat	Trauma, insufficient calcium in diet, chewing objects that are too hard
Cancer	Illness, lack of appetite, weight loss, depression, inactivity, sometimes visible lumps	Old age, viral disease; some cancers are possibly inherited
Cataracts	Cataracts (cloudy lens) due to improper diet, diabetes, or genetic factors	Diabetes, incorrect diet, possible genetic inheritance
Constipation	Straining to pass hard, dry feces or inability to pass feces; depression, lethargy, hunched-up position, dry, ruffled fur	Insufficient water intake, dehydration, heat, illness, intestinal obstruction, parasitism
Dehydration	Skin is stiff, and lacks elasticity—when pulled it stands up and is slow to fall back in place, animal is lethargic and weak	Bacterial or viral infections and diseases, stress, improper diet, heatstroke
Dental malocclusion	Protruding or misdirected front teeth, lack of appetite, inability to eat, weight loss, swollen, painful mouth, infection	Possibly inherited condition, may also be due to trauma or injury
Diarrhea	Soft, mucus, or liquid feces, odor, wet around anus, dehydration, lack of appetite, weight loss, lethargy, hunched-up position	Can be caused by protozoan disease *Giardia*, bacterial or viral infections, stress, improper diet

Do	*Don't*
Cleanse wounds with antiseptic, hydrogen peroxide, keep clean, allow to drain	Do not overcrowd or house animals that are not compatible with each other
Emergency situation, death can result quickly, check with veterinarian to see if treatment with 25 mg/kg fenbendazole for 5 days is indicated	Do not wait, do not stress, do not handle
Continue to trim tooth opposite broken tooth until broken tooth grows and both teeth mesh properly	Do not allow the opposite tooth to grow into soft tissues of the mouth
Keep pet comfortable, seek veterinary help to treat symptoms	Do not try to prolong animal's life if animal is very ill and suffering
Consult veterinarian. No cure available	Do not change degu's environment; adapting to change can be stressful for a blind animal
Determine cause, increase fluid intake, check for possible bowel obstruction and parasites, check with veterinarian to see if mineral oil enema is indicated	Do not allow access to foreign material that can cause intestinal obstruction (plastic), avoid hot, dry areas
Consult veterinarian, rehydrate, determine cause of problem, remove from heat if applicable	Do not handle more than necessary, do not stress, do not give homemade salt and sugar mixtures that are not correctly balanced
Use animal nail clippers to trim teeth back to correct and even length; check and trim teeth regularly for entire life	Do not use in breeding program
Contact veterinarian to determine cause, rehydrate immediately, isolate from other animals, allow sufficient time to recover	Avoid handling any more than necessary, do not stress, do not feed fruits or diets high in sugar content

(continued on page 78)

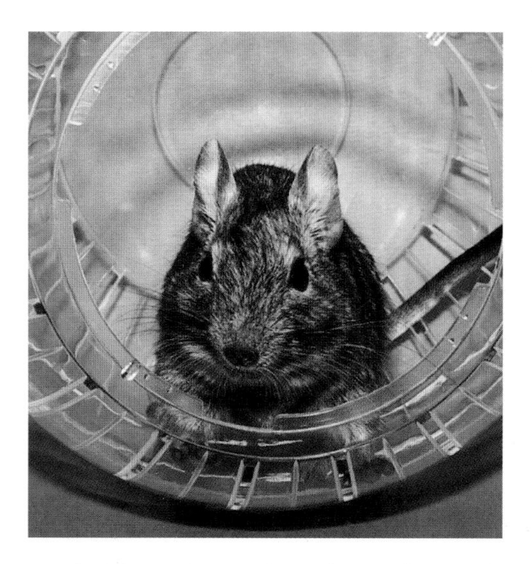

Degus can easily be stepped on and injured. A safe way to let your degu explore outside of its cage without risk of injury by feet or household pets is by supervising it in a hamster ball.

Resistance and Sensitivity to Medications

Degus are resistant to some kinds of medications and sensitive to others.

Use only medicines prescribed for your degu by your veterinarian and give no more than the recommended dose.

✔ *Never give your degu any medicine intended for you or your other pets.*

Sensitivity to High Elevations

You might think that because the degu comes from the Andes in South America, it lives at high altitudes. Remember that the degu lives in the foothills of the west slopes of the Andes, up to an elevation of about 3,900 feet (1,200 m), and not at the peaks. In fact, degus are poorly adapted to high elevations because they do not have the ability to change the concentration of red blood cells or hemoglobin (blood components necessary for oxygen transport) when they are suddenly exposed to high altitudes. The degu is not unique is this regard—most rodents do not have this ability either.

Zoonotic Diseases

Zoonotic diseases are diseases that can be shared between animals and humans. Many species of animals are carriers of certain diseases that do not make them ill, but can make people very sick. Likewise, people can carry germs to which they are resistant, but that adversely affect certain animal species. Some disease organisms cause illness in both humans and animals.

Wild degus in Chile have been known to carry three diseases contagious to humans:

✔ *Linguatula serrata*—a worm that lives in the sinuses and nasal passages of some animal species and can parasitize humans.

✔ *Echinococcus granulosus*—a small tapeworm that parasitizes different animal species and can form cysts in various organs of the body.

✔ *Trympanosoma cruzi*—a protozoan that can live in animals and be transmitted to humans through the bite of a specific bug.

It is highly unlikely that your domestic pet degu would be carrying any of these diseases.

If your degu becomes ill, your veterinarian can answer questions you may have about the contagion of different diseases or parasites.

Euthanasia

When It's Time to Say Good-bye

Even with the best care in the world, your degu will someday develop signs of old age or illness. This will be a difficult time for your pet, because it will not be able to run and play and enjoy life as it did when it was younger and healthy. It will also be an emotionally painful time for you, because you will feel helpless in your inability to prevent or cure the problem, and you will not want your small friend to suffer even for a moment. At some point in time you will ask the question: should my pet be euthanized?

Euthanasia means putting an animal to death humanely, peacefully, and painlessly. There are different ways veterinarians euthanize animals, depending on the circumstances. Euthanasia is usually done by first giving the animal a sedative to make it sleep deeply and then giving it a lethal substance by injection that ends its life almost instantly.

If you are asking yourself whether your pet should be euthanized, there must be good reasons. The decision of when to euthanize is a difficult one that depends upon many things. A good rule of thumb is if your pet's suffering cannot be relieved, if your pet's quality of life is poor, or if the "bad days" simply outnumber the "good days" for your pet, it is time to seriously consider euthanasia. Your veterinarian can answer any specific questions you or your family may have. Your veterinarian can also help you if you wish to find a pet cemetery or have your pet cremated.

During this emotional time, remember to take care of yourself and allow time to grieve. If you have children in the family, deal with the issue of animal loss at a level they can understand, comfort them, and let them share their grief. (See Children and Degus). Take comfort in the knowledge you took good care of your pet throughout its life and that you made the best decisions regarding its health and welfare, even when you had to make the most difficult decision of all.

A comfortable home, companionship, and a treat. Degus are easy to please!

Degu Health Check Sheet (continued from page 75)

Health Problem	*Symptoms*	*Causes*
Ear problems	Scratching, head shaking, loss of balance, pain	Parasites, infection, injury, disease
Eye problems	Discharge (runny eyes)—either clear or viscous, closed eyes, dull or cloudy eyes	Infection, injury, irritating substances, disease
Heatstroke	Hot, weak, unresponsive, comatose, may appear to be dead	Exposure to high temperatures, inadequate ventilation
Infections	Symptoms vary according to organism and type of infection, severe illness and death from bacteria *Pseudomonas* found in contaminated water	Bacteria, viruses, fungi, protozoa
Nails	Torn nail may bleed, become infected and interfere with activities	Injury
Respiratory problems	Wheezing, sneezing, difficulty breathing, discharge from nose and eyes, lack of appetite, inactivity, weight loss	Viral, fungal, or bacterial infection, allergies, exposure to fine dusts, exposure to drafts or cold, damp, environment
Skin and fur problems	Loss of fur, sores, flaky or moist skin, redness, oozing, itching, scratching, infection	Bacterial or fungal infections, parasitism, improper diet, allergies, disease, hormonal imbalance
Teeth	Teeth that are pale yellow or white in color indicate poor health	Yellow teeth may be due to dietary deficiency or illness
Trauma	Inactivity, lack of appetite, inability to walk or sit normally, broken bones, bleeding, swelling, pain	Numerous possibilities, including being dropped, stepped on, and bitten

Do	*Don't*
Consult veterinarian to determine cause of problem	Do not handle any more than necessary, especially around the head and ears
Place degu in a dark area, isolate from other animals, consult veterinarian for diagnosis, eye problems can be very painful	Avoid light, which can be painful to the injured eye; do not handle more than necessary, do not stress
Remove from hot area, hold in hand and submerge body in cool water while keeping head above water, dry well and rehydrate as soon as pet is conscious	Do not handle more than necessary, do not stress, allow to recover in safe, dark place
Consult your veterinarian	Do not allow problem to progress or animal to suffer
Provide soft bedding and footrests, keep injury clean to prevent infection, if animal is in pain or infection develops, notify veterinarian	Do not trim torn nail too close to base of nail—this may worsen the problem
Contact your veterinarian immediately before problem develops into pneumonia, which can result in death, isolate from other pets	Do not expose pet to cold or damp environment or dusty cage material, do not handle more than necessary, do not stress
Contact your veterinarian for diagnosis and medication, keep skin and fur clean	Do not put drying products on dry skin, nor moisturizers on moist skin without first consulting a veterinarian
Consult veterinarian to determine cause and treatment	Do not disregard problem or animal may die
Observe closely to determine extent of injury; isolate from other pets, contact veterinarian	Do not house with other animals, do not handle any more than necessary, do not stress

RAISING DEGUS

Raising degus is relatively easy. It is also a lot of fun. But you will encounter some challenges along the way and there are some important facts you must know to be successful at this new hobby.

One of the most interesting facts about degu reproduction is that the degu has a relatively long gestation period, 90 days, as compared to other rodents (for example, hamsters have a gestation period of 16 to 18 days). Degus also reach sexual maturity much later than many rodents.

What does all this mean to you as a budding degu breeder? For one thing, you need to pay close attention to your degus so you will know when to plan for a litter. Before you breed your degus, make sure that you have good homes lined up for the babies when they are ready to leave the nest.

If you do not want your degus to breed, separate the males from the females at the time of weaning. Same-sex degu siblings will live together peacefully if you keep them housed together from the time they are weaned.

At the slightest sound, the male degu will pop his head out to investigate, keeping his mate and offspring tucked away safely in the nest box.

Reproductive Characteristics

Degus have some unusual reproductive characteristics that deserve discussion at this point.

Females: The female degu has eight nipples. One pair is located in the inguinal area and three pairs are located along the sides of the thorax and abdomen. The position of the nipples makes it possible for the mother to huddle the babies and for the babies to lie on their backs while they suckle.

✔ The degu has a bicornate uterus. That means that from the cervix, the uterus branches into a Y-shape, consisting of a left and a right uterine horn. This conformation enables the mother to carry several offspring in each of the elongated uterine horns.

✔ The female degu has a large clitoris that is sometimes mistaken for a penis by inexperienced degu owners.

✔ All female mammals are born with a vaginal membrane that remains closed until puberty (sexual maturity) is reached. In the degu, this membrane opens during estrus, closes after mating, and may open and close sporadically during gestation. It reopens at the time of partuition (giving birth).

Males: The testicles of male degus are retained inguinally or in the abdominal cavity and there is no scrotum. The degu's penis is directed posteriorly and is covered with tiny spines (spicules). It is believed the spicules serve to stimulate ovulation in the female when breeding takes place.

Upon ejaculation (the release of sperm during breeding), the secretions of reproductive accessory glands and the prostate gland mix with the semen and form a mixture that forms a small plug, called a "copulatory plug," that may be visible at the entry to the female degu's vagina shortly after breeding. The copulatory plug is a useful indicator that mating has occurred.

The Reproductive Cycle

In the wild, female degus are seasonal breeders. This means they only breed during a certain time of the year. It is interesting to note that male degus are not seasonal breeders. They are fertile year-round and able to breed at any time.

In their native habitat in central Chile, degus breed in September, corresponding with the last of the rainy season and the month of greatest plant growth. This seasonality ensures that the baby degus will be born in a time of food abundance. In the northern parts of the degu's range, the breeding season may extend from November to April. In captivity in the northern hemisphere, degus have been observed to breed year-round, with the most litters produced in December, July, and August, and the fewest births in April, May, and June. This means the most fertile breedings take place in September, October, April, May, and June.

As a degu breeder, you need to closely observe your degus, particularly during the breeding season. That way you can prepare for a possible litter well in advance.

Puberty

Unlike many rodents, degus take a long time to reach sexual maturity. They may reach puberty at 6 months of age, but an average age range of 14 to 20 months is not unusual. Most females have attained a weight of 7 ounces (200 g) by the time of their first conception (when pregnancy takes place).

Estrus

Degus do not have a regular estrous cycle. They are "induced ovulators." This means breeding must take place in order to stimulate ovulation (the release of eggs from the ovaries). Estrus is the time during the breeding season that the female degu will permit the male to mate with her. Estrus is the time period just before and just after ovulation.

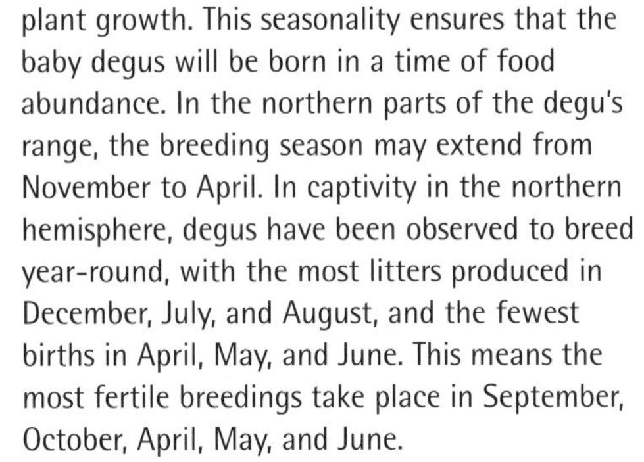

The male degu initiates courtship by nuzzling, trembling, wagging, and grooming the female.

Enurination, or urine spraying, is a normal part of the degu courtship ritual.

Signs of estrus in the female degu can be subtle and difficult to detect. She may show some slight swelling of the vulva and an opening in the vaginal membrane may also be noted. Female degus usually exhibit a rise in activity level on the day of estrus and a slight increase in body temperature (normal body temperature is 101.8°F [37.9°C]).

Estrus in the degu lasts only three hours, so the male degu has a small window of opportunity in which to work. Because estrus may be difficult to detect, if you want to be sure your degus have an opportunity to breed, house the male and female together at all times. This is a more natural living arrangement for their well-being and it allows time for them to bond. Even if you are not sure when the female came into estrus, the male will detect when the female is ready to breed and he will begin his courtship behavior. Although estrus in the degu is very short, the mating act (copulation) takes even less time, approximately ten seconds. The vaginal membrane closes shortly after breeding.

Courtship Behavior

During the breeding season, the male degu will initiate courtship. This behavior includes grooming the female, tail-wagging, nose-to-nose contact, nuzzling, and trembling.

Enurination: A peculiar part of the courtship behavior involves scent-marking by urine spraying, called enurination. The male will lift a hind leg over the back of the female and spray urine. The female will sometimes return the gesture. Enurination is believed to serve as an odor-distributing mechanism that familiarizes the male with the female and promotes increased tolerance. In this manner, the male courtship behavior is a means to appease the female and attain access to her.

As the courting ritual continues, the male will attempt to mount the female. If she is not yet receptive, her behavior can be unpredictable. She might resist or withdraw from the male or she may threaten and lunge at him. When the female is in estrus and ready to accept the male, he will mount and breed her.

Breeding takes place quickly, in five to ten seconds. It has been suggested that the short time necessary for mating has evolved as an antipredator defense mechanism. If degus spent too much time mating, they would be distracted and unaware of predators in the area. This would make them more vulnerable to attacks.

After mating, the male will make loud, characteristic, repetitive squeaks, one to three seconds apart. This postcopulatory vocalization is

Lateral nipples are easy to find on this lactating mother degu.

prolonged and may last as long as five to six minutes after the first breeding. The call appears to be a warning to other male degus in the area, telling them to stay away. After all, if another male breeds the same female during the three-hour estrous period, the first male may end up raising some babies that are not his own! Several matings can take place while the female is in estrus. The male's postcopulatory calls become even more prolonged after subsequent matings, sometimes lasting as long as 18 minutes.

Ovulation

Ovulation is the release of eggs from the ovaries. Assuming the male is fertile, the number of young conceived will depend upon the number of eggs released during ovulation, which usually range from zero to ten, with an average of five to six.

Implantation

Implantation, the attachment of the embryo to the uterus, takes place in the degu six to seven days after mating. The placenta is an organ that attaches the fetuses to the mother's uterus so that they can receive nutrition. Placentation in the degu is different from other rodents or mammalian species. In technical terms it is called an allanto-chorionic subplacenta, and to our knowledge, exists only in degus.

Unlike some mammalian species, delayed implantation and delayed fertilization do not occur in the degu.

Pregnancy

The time during which the female is pregnant, that is, from conception to birth, is called gestation. The 90-day (87- to 93-day range) gestation period in the degu is very long compared to most rodents. Usually, a long gestation means the offspring are born precocious, that is, well developed and fully able to fend for themselves. While it is true that degus are born with fur and their eyes open (in some colonies eyes open at two to three days of age), newborn degus are not fully coordinated and are not able to protect themselves. They rely on their parents for nutrition, protection, and warmth because they cannot maintain their own body warmth (thermoregulate) until they are eight days of age.

So if the baby degus are not precocious, why is the gestation period so long? Researchers attribute the prolonged gestation to the degu's unusual type of placentation. Studies indicate that 25 percent of the gestation period is due to the proliferation of placental tissues and slow fetal growth.

Another theory has been postulated to account for the degu's long gestation. Species with long life spans and long reproductive periods have large brains at birth and in adulthood. It has been suggested that the gestation length is determined by the brain weight and stage of development at birth.

If your degu is carrying several young, you will probably detect an increase in size in her abdomen during the last month of her pregnancy and when you pick her up you may notice she feels heavier.

If you think your degu is pregnant, handle her carefully and gently. Be careful of the unborn babies and do not grasp the mother-to-be too firmly around her abdomen. Do not make changes in her nest box or cage and do not remove her mate. Remember that degus bond closely to one another and participate together in raising the babies. Your degus will become stressed and very depressed if they are separated.

Birth (Parturition)

Your degu will give birth in her nest box. She may require a few hours to deliver the entire litter. During parturition, resist the temptation to peek into the nest box too frequently, as this can stress or frighten the parents.

Degu parents are very protective of their young. It is very unlikely that they will bite you if you reach into the nest box, but be sensitive to their feelings. If they are upset they will growl or if they are very fearful they will make cries and whimpering sounds similar to a puppy. During the first few hours after birth it is best to leave the nest box and the new family alone.

Soon after birth, the female degu will come into estrus again. This is called a postpartum estrus. This early estrus is not uncommon in rodent species. However, unlike many rodents, degus usually do not breed on their postpartum estrus. Degus that are kept in captivity are subjected to artificial lighting and this may affect whether or not postpartum breeding occurs (see Degu Reproduction Chart).

Parental Care

Parental care begins long before the babies are born. It begins with the strong bond between the parents that ensures the two will work together to raise the litter. Sometimes animals are inadvertently separated after breeding, particularly in captivity where a pregnant female may be separated from her mate and

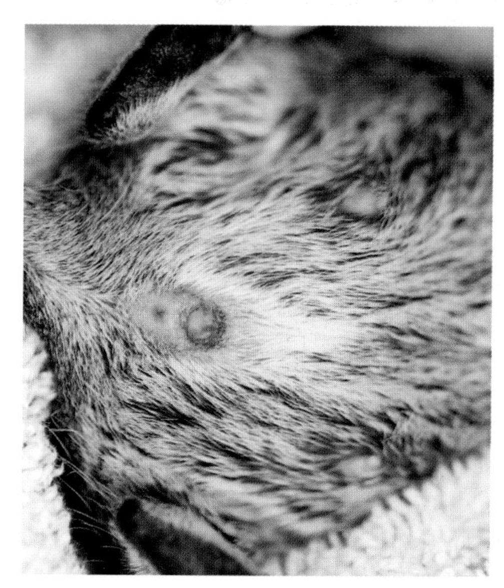

Enlarged inguinal nipples and vaginal membrane are evident on this pregnant degu.

Degu Reproduction

Breeding Season	
In captivity	Year round Fewest births in April, May, June
In native Chile	November through April
Estrous cycle	No regular estrous cycle
Duration of estrus	Approximately 3 hours
Induced ovulator	Yes
Implantation	7 days after fertilization takes place
Gestation	90 days (87 to 92 days)
Litter size	4 to 6 young (average 5.3)
Litters/year	1 to 2
Breed on postpartum estrus	Sometimes*
Weight at birth	14 g
Born with fur and eyes open	Yes**
Ability to thermoregulate	8 days of age
Weaning	5 to 6 weeks of age
Sexual maturity (puberty)	6 to 20 months of age, (63 days minimum)
Weight at first conception	205 g (7.2 ounces)

*Although the scientific literature states that it is unusual for degus to breed on their postpartum estrus, it has been the author's experience that if degus are subjected to light 24 hours per day, they will breed on the postpartum estrus. Degus in the wild would not be subjected to these artificial conditions.
** Degus born in the United States are more developed at birth than degus born in the United Kingdom. Degus in the United States are born with their eyes open and almost, if not entirely, fully furred. Degus in the United Kingdom are born with sparse fur and closed eyes, which open in one to two days. The reasons for these differences in development at birth are not known at present, but may be an indication of genetic variation in the foundation animals originally exported from South America decades ago.

sold as a pet. Male degus are dedicated mates and fathers. If the pregnant female finds another male with which to bond, her new mate will raise and protect the litter, although he is not the true father.

Degu parents will build a nest in anticipation of the impending birth. If you suspect your degu is pregnant, be sure to provide her with a nest box and fresh grass or hay so she and her mate can build a clean, warm, comfortable nest.

Baby degus depend on their parents for survival. The mother and father take turns huddling the babies and keeping them warm. In some cases, the mother huddles the young only when she nurses and the father huddles the young the rest of the time. The baby degus absorb body heat from their parents. As the babies grow, they become less dependent on their parents for body heat. By the time they are eight days of age they can create and maintain their own body warmth.

Mother degus nurse their babies in a huddled position. Baby degus lie on their backs to suckle.

Nursing

Mother degus nurse their young by standing and huddling over them. The babies lay on their backs underneath her to suckle. As the babies grow larger, they may suckle on their stomachs or their backs. Eventually, when they grow stronger, they may force their mother onto her side while being nursed.

Degus nurse for an average of 25 minutes. During this time the babies often change nipples. In some of the other Hystricomorph rodent species, suckling time is brief and the babies claim ownership of a given nipple, suckling from the same nipple during each nursing bout. A reduction in nursing time is believed to have evolved in animals that live in unprotected areas and are more susceptible to predation. These animals cannot risk taking a long time to eat out in the open where they might be attacked. Because degus live in protected underground burrows, they have developed a behavior that enables the mother and babies to take more time for meals and establish close family bonds.

Degu Growth Chart

	Weight		*Body Length (nose to rump)*	
Age	*Males*	*Females*	*Males*	*Females*
Birth	.56 oz (16 g)	1/2 oz (14 g)	2.6 inches (65 mm)	2 inches (50 mm)
21 days/3 weeks	2.1 oz (60 g)	2 oz (56 g)	4 inches (100 mm)	3.5 inches (90 mm)
28 days/4 weeks	2.5 oz (72 g)	2.3 oz (66 g)	4.1 inches (105 mm)	4 inches (100 mm)
35 days/5 weeks	3.2 oz (92 g)	2.8 oz (80 g)	4.3 inches (110 mm)	4.1 inches (105 mm)
42 days/6 weeks	4 oz (114 g)	3.5 oz (100 g)	4.9 inches (125 mm)	4.5 inches (115 mm)
49 days/7 weeks	4.3 oz (123 g)	4 oz (113 g)	5.5 inches (140 mm)	5.1 inches (130 mm)
56 days/8 weeks	4.7 oz (135 g)	4.3 oz (123 g)	6.5 inches (165 mm)	6.1 inches (155 mm)
63 days/9 weeks	5 oz (145 g)	4.5 oz (130 g)	7.3 inches (185 mm)	6.9 inches (175 mm)
70 days/10 weeks	5.4 oz (153 g)	4.8 oz (137 g)	8.2 inches (210 mm)	7.8 inches (200 mm)
Adult	7–14 oz (200–400 g)	6–10.5 oz (170–300 g)	11.8 inches (300 mm)	9.8 inches (250 mm)

A large, round body are tell-tale signs of pregnancy in this female, who is due to give birth in the next few days. Most pregnant degus are larger than male degus.

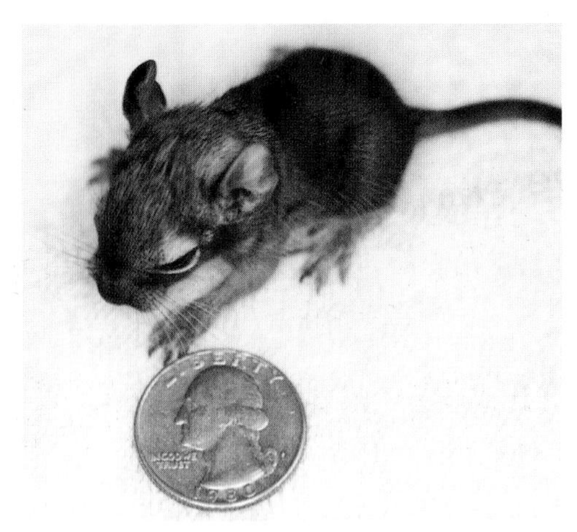

This tiny newborn degu weighs only 1/2 ounce (15 g) and will take from 6 to 20 months to reach sexual maturity.

The male degu spends most of his time guarding the nest box during the female's pregnancy.

Paternal Care

When the father is not huddling the babies, he is grooming the mother or standing guard over the nest. In captivity, the male spends long hours guarding the nest box with his head sticking out, letting out warning squeaks at the slightest disturbance.

Unlike some Hystricomorph rodents, father degus do not enurinate on the young degus. It is believed that the male accepts the young because they smell similar to their mother. Father degus rarely, if ever, engage in play with the babies.

Birth Announcements

Degu parents have special calls they use to communicate with their babies from birth. Baby degus make two distinct sounds at birth: a peeping or whistling sound and a chattering sound.

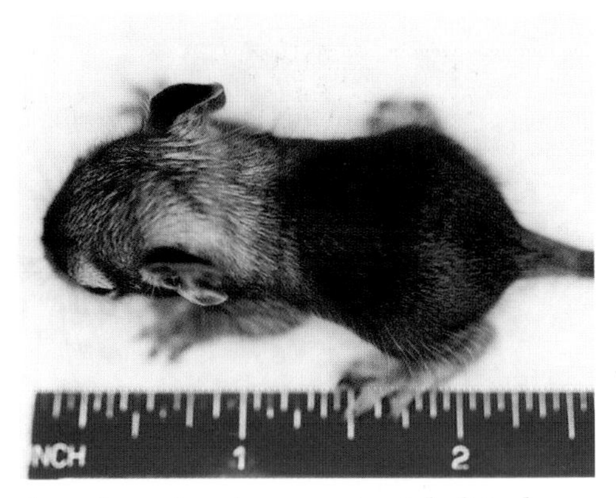

A newborn degu is approximately 2 inches (50 mm) in length. Note the scant amount of fur on the rump of this youngster.

The degu's large head size may be a contributing factor to the long gestation period.

If you think your degu may have had babies, but you don't want to disturb the nest box, listen closely for soft sounds resembling little birds chirping. You will recognize these tender sounds as the announcement of the birth of a new litter!

Lactation

Lactation is the production of milk by the mammary glands or breasts. The composition of milk, its percentage of fat, protein, and water varies for each species. Lactation is a unique feature of all mammals. It makes it possible for mother animals to nourish their immature young safely in hiding, anytime, anywhere. It is a practical approach to increase survival of offspring during times of food shortage.

When a mother is lactating, she is turning the food she has eaten and the fat she has stored into milk for her babies. This process requires energy and burns up calories. It makes it necessary for the mother to eat more food and drink more water than usual.

Degus produce body heat when they lactate. This body heat helps keep the pups warm. Mother degus may lose weight during lactation. Be sure to provide lots of nutritious food and plenty of water during that time.

The average degu litter size is five. These newborns are quite a handful!

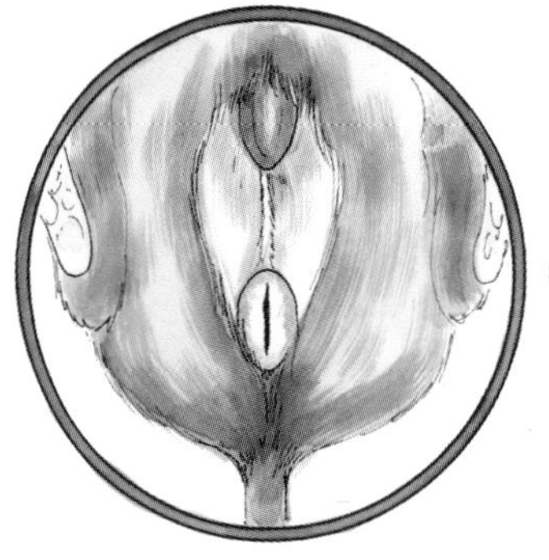

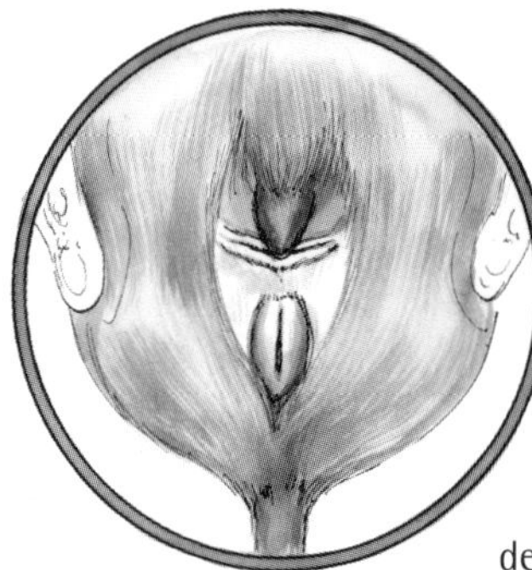

In male degus, the distance from the anus to the urethral orifice is greater than in female degus.

Weaning

A weaned animal is an animal that no longer requires and is no longer receiving nourishment from its mother's milk. Degu babies can eat small amounts of solid food within a few days of birth, but they cannot survive without their mother's milk until they are at least two weeks of age. Baby degus should not be weaned from their mother earlier than four weeks of age and ideally around six weeks of age.

In the wild, degu mothers nurse their litters for several weeks. This prolonged nursing period allows the mother and young to form a close bond. The young degus will continue to suckle although they no longer require their mother's milk to survive. The mother will continue to nurse her young while they are juveniles at risk of predation and unable to assume adult roles. By remaining with their family, the young degus benefit from the food, housing, and protection provided by their parents.

Baby Degu Development and Behavior

Activity	*Age*
Walks	1 day
Washes face, licks paws, and grooms itself	1 day
Scratches itself with hind feet	2 days
Licks and washes	3 days
Sits upright	4 days
Runs and jumps	5 days
Washes fur on belly	6 days
Spends most of the time playing	8 days
Takes dust baths	14 days
Stands up, gurgles, and paws at littermates	14 days

Imprinting and Taming

Imprinting is what takes place when a very young animal sees another animal and immediately forms a close bond with it. In the wild, baby animals almost always imprint on their mothers. She is the first thing they see, smell, hear, and recognize. They depend on her for protection. They follow her and learn from her. The same is true for degus. By the time you are able to handle the babies safely, they will have already imprinted on their mother.

This in no way interferes with your ability to tame your baby degu. Degus are gentle animals that are very easy to tame. Regular handling will make it an affectionate and enjoyable pet. The degu babies will quickly recognize you as a friend and provider of food and look forward to your visits.

Raising Baby Degus

Once you wean the young degus, they can be housed just like the adults. They have the same needs: nutritious food, fresh water, an exercise wheel, interesting toys, comfortable temperature, safe, escape-proof housing, and lots of attention.

Regular handling is an important part of keeping your pet tame. Young degus are naturally friendly. They are also curious and love to investigate. Sometimes your degu will want to explore; other times it will want to be held and caressed. Your degus will be a continual source of fun and entertainment for you and the more time you spend with them, the more affectionate they will be.

Sexing Baby Degus

It is not difficult to determine the sex of the baby degus at an early age. Hold the baby carefully, belly up, with its back against the palm of your hand. You may hold the tail gently, but do not pull on it. Once you have identified the anus, located under the tail, proceed upwards to the genital opening. The distance between the anus and the urethral orifice, or the anogenital distance, is greater in males than in females. Female degus have a small anatomical structure, a clitoris, that can be mistaken for a penis. By comparing the littermates to each other and noting the anogenital distance, you will quickly learn to identify the males from the females.

The Babies Leave Home

As tempting as it is, you probably will not keep every baby degu you raise. As a responsible degu breeder you will be sure that the youngsters are going to loving homes where they will receive good care.

To be sure everything goes well for the degus, provide the new owners with as much information as you can about their care. Show them the type of cage you use to house your degus. Demonstrate how to pick up the animals and examine them. Give the new owners a bag of the food you are currently feeding. This will prevent the stress of a change in diet. And finally, in case of a problem, recommend any veterinarians you know who have a special interest in pocket pets.

By now you have gained quite a bit of knowledge about degus. So you will surely agree that the only difficult thing about raising degus is parting with the babies!

Degus are excellent parents.

INFORMATION

Organizations

American Society of Mammologists
H. Duane Smith, Secretary-Treasurer
Monte L. Bean Life Sciences Museum
Brigham Young University
Provo, UT 84602-0200
http://asm.wku.edu

American Veterinary Medical Association
1931 N. Meacham Road
Suite 100
Schaumberg, IL 60173-4360
(847) 925-8070
www.avma.org

Additional Reading

Fulk, G. W. "Notes on the Activity, Reproduction, and Social Behavior of *Octodon degus*." Journal of Mammology, Vol 57, No 3, August 1976.

The Biology of Hystricomorph Rodents, The Proceedings of a Symposium Held at the Zoological Society of London, Ed. Rowlands, I. W., and Weir, B. J. Published for the Zoological Society of London by Academic Press, 1974.

Woods, C. A., and Boraker, D. K. 1975. "Octodon degus." *Mammalian Species*, 67: 1–5.

Important Note

This pet owner's guide tells the reader how to buy and care for degus. The advice given in the book applies to healthy animals with good dispositions obtained from a reputable source. Extraordinary efforts have been made by the author and the publisher to insure that treatment recommendations are precise and in agreement with standards accepted at the time of publication. If your degu exhibits any signs of illness you should consult a veterinarian immediately—some diseases are dangerous for human beings. If you have any questions about an illness, or if you have been scratched or bitten by your degu, consult a physician immediately. Some people are allergic to animal hair, dander, saliva, urine, and feces; are immune-suppressed; or are immunologically compromised, and cannot be exposed to animals. If you are not sure, consult your physician before you acquire a degu.

Be sure to instruct children in the safe handling of degus and supervise children when they are handling degus. Never leave your pets or small children alone with degus.

If your degu escapes, to prevent electrical accidents, be sure your degu cannot gnaw on electrical wires and remember your degu may cause you to fall if it runs between your feet and you are trying not to step on it.

The author and publisher assume no responsibility for and make no warranty with respect to results that may be obtained from procedures cited. Neither the author nor the publisher shall be liable for any damage resulting from reliance on any information contained herein, whether with respect to procedures, or by reason of any misstatement, error, or omission, negligent or otherwise, contained in this work. Information contained herein is presented as a reference only and is not a substitution for consultation with veterinarians or physicians.

INDEX

About the Author

Sharon Vanderlip, D.V.M., has provided veterinary care to exotic and domestic animal species for more than 20 years. She has written books and articles in scientific and lay publications. Dr. Vanderlip served as the Associate Director of Veterinary Services for the University of California at San Diego School of Medicine, has worked on collaborative projects with the Zoological Society of San Diego, has owned her own veterinary practice, is former Chief of Veterinary Services for the National Aeronautics and Space Administration (NASA), and is a consultant for wildlife projects. She has a special fondness for degus, especially her own!

Photo Credits

Zig Leszczynski: pages 2-3, 4, 5, 8 top, 8 bottom, 9, 12 top, 12 bottom, 13 top, 13 bottom, 16, 17, 20 left, 20 right, 21, 24 top, 25 left, 25 right, 28, 29, 32 top, 32 bottom, 33, 37, 40, 41, 44 top, 44 bottom, 45 top, 45 bottom, 48, 49 left, 49 right, 56, 57, 60 top, 60 bottom, 61 top, 61 bottom left, 61 bottom right, 64, 65, 68, 69 left, 69 right, 73 top right, 73 bottom right, 77, 80, 81, 88 bottom left, 92 left, 92 right, 93; Sharon Vanderlip: pages 24 bottom, 36, 52, 53 top, 53 bottom, 72, 73 top left, 76, 84, 85, 88 top left, 88 top right, 89 top left, 89 top right, 89 bottom right.

Cover Photos

All covers by Zig Leszczynski.

Acknowledgments

I would like to thank my husband, Jack Vanderlip, D.V.M., for his invaluable help as an expert consultant in laboratory and exotic animal medicine. His behind-the-scenes activities included obtaining hard-to-find scientific resources and critically reviewing the final manuscript. I am especially appreciative of his enthusiastic support and genuine interest in my work. I would also like to thank our daughter, Jacquelynn, for her help caring for the degus and for her patience and assistance during degu photo sessions. The encouragement and enthusiasm of these two special people contributed significantly to the quality of the manuscript.

All inquiries should be addressed to:
Barron's Educational Series, Inc.
250 Wireless Boulevard
Hauppauge, NY 11788
http://www.barronseduc.com

International Standard Book No. 0-7641-1600-2

Library of Congress Catalog Card No. 00-034215

Library of Congress Cataloging-in-Publication Data
Vanderlip, Sharon Lynn.
Degus / Sharon Vanderlip.
p. cm. — (A Complete pet owner's manual)
Includes bibliographical references (p.).
ISBN 0-7641-1600-2 (alk. paper)
1. Degus as pets. I. Title. II. Series.
SF459.D43 V36 2001
636.9'35—dc21 00-034215

Printed in Hong Kong

9 8 7 6 5 4 3 2 1